W9-BFY-461

Mark Twain

Banned, Challenged, and Censored

Titles in the *Authors of Banned Books* series:

J. K. Rowling
Banned, Challenged, and Censored

ISBN-13: 978-0-7660-2687-2
ISBN-10: 0-7660-2687-6

John Steinbeck
Banned, Challenged, and Censored

ISBN-13: 978-0-7660-2688-9
ISBN-10: 0-7660-2688-4

Madeleine L'Engle
Banned, Challenged, and Censored

ISBN-13: 978-0-7660-2708-4
ISBN-10: 0-7660-2708-2

Mark Twain
Banned, Challenged, and Censored

ISBN-13: 978-0-7660-2689-6
ISBN-10: 0-7660-2689-2

Robert Cormier
Banned, Challenged, and Censored

ISBN-13: 978-0-7660-2691-9
ISBN-10: 0-7660-2691-4

Authors of **Banned Books**

Mark Twain

Banned, Challenged, and Censored

Michelle M. Houle

Enslow Publishers, Inc.
40 Industrial Road
Box 398
Berkeley Heights, NJ 07922
USA

http://www.enslow.com

TALCOTT
LIBRARY

To Scott and Addie, and our life less ordinary.

Copyright © 2008 by Michelle M. Houle

All rights reserved.

No part of this book may be reproduced by any means without the written permission of the publisher.

Library of Congress Cataloging-in-Publication Data

Houle, Michelle M.
  Mark Twain : banned, challenged, and censored / Michelle M. Houle.
    p. cm.—(Authors of banned books)
  Summary: "Examines the life of Mark Twain, his most famous literary works, and the controversy his literature has created in schools and libraries"—Provided by publisher.
  Includes bibliographical references and index.
  ISBN-13: 978-0-7660-2689-6
  ISBN-10: 0-7660-2689-2
  1. Twain, Mark, 1835-1910—Criticism and interpretation—Juvenile literature. 2. Twain, Mark, 1835-1910—Censorship—Juvenile literature. 3. Challenged books—Juvenile literature. 4. Prohibited books—Juvenile literature. 5. Censorship—Juvenile literature. I. Title.
  PS1338.H66 2008
  818'.409—dc22
                              2007022362

Printed in the United States of America

10 9 8 7 6 5 4 3 2 1

To Our Readers: We have done our best to make sure that all Internet addresses in this book were active and appropriate when we went to press. However, the author and publisher have no control over and assume no liability for the material available on those Internet sites or on other Web sites they may link to. Any comments or suggestions can be sent by e-mail to comments@enslow.com or to the address on the back cover.

Illustration Credits: AP/Wide World, pp. 33, 109; reproduced from the *Dictionary of American Portraits*, published by Dover Publications, Inc., in 1967, p. 102; Digital Vision, p. 130; Library of Congress, pp. 1, 19, 52, 59, 65, 74, 81, 92; Office for Intellectual Freedom, American Library Association, p. 121; Photos.com, p. 115.

Cover Illustration: Library of Congress.

Contents

Chapter 1

Concord, Massachusetts, 1885, vs. Enid, Oklahoma, 2000

Vulgarity. Poor grammar. Low morals. Heresy. Nudity. Sexism. Racism.

These are some of the frequent objections to *Adventures of Huckleberry Finn* by Mark Twain (the pen name of Samuel Clemens), one of the most controversial books of all time. For more than a century, it has been challenged, banned, burned, and removed from libraries and classrooms across the country.

Despite this, the novel is also often considered a classic icon of American literature. The famous author Ernest Hemingway even wrote:

All modern American literature comes from one book by Mark Twain called *Huckleberry Finn*.... [I]t's the best book we've had. All American writing comes from that. There was nothing before. There has been nothing as good since.[1]

How can one book cause such violently different reactions?

1885: Concord, Massachusetts

The year was 1885, and Mark Twain's new novel, *Adventures of Huckleberry Finn*, was finally in print. For months, readers had been offered glimpses of the tale in short extracts in magazines, but the novel's full publication had been continually delayed. When it was finally available in February, readers could read the book in its entirety for the first time. For many, this experience was a shock. What was this coarse language, unruly behavior, petty thievery, and even murder doing in a novel marketed as the companion book to *The Adventures of Tom Sawyer*, a beloved "boy's book" ultimately enjoyed by children and adults alike?

The library committee of Concord, Massachusetts, was not impressed by the newest offering from Mark Twain, the pseudonym, or pen name, of Samuel L. Clemens, who was already a famous writer and lecturer by this time. Despite this fame—or perhaps because of it—the committee was particularly keen to make a point with their response to *Huckleberry Finn*. Thus, in

8

Concord, Massachusetts, 1885, vs. Enid, Oklahoma, 2000

March of 1885, just a few weeks after the first printing of the novel, the library removed the book from its shelves, calling it "trash of the veriest sort."[2]

At first, Twain was amused. He joked that the ban, and the stories about it which were published in newspapers all around the country, would boost sales of the novel significantly in the end. He wrote:

> [The ban] will deter other libraries from buying the book and you are doubtless aware that one book in a public library prevents the sale of a sure ten and a possible hundred of its mates. And secondly it will cause the purchasers of the book to read it, out of curiosity, instead of merely intending to do so after the usual way of the world and library committees; and then they will discover, to my great advantage and their own indignant disappointment, that there is nothing objectionable in the book, after all.[3]

More than one hundred twenty years after the first publication of *Adventures of Huckleberry Finn*, the debate over the novel's status on the library shelf continues, though now it is sometimes for very different reasons. For example, Twain was originally criticized for having his characters speak with "improper" grammar. Now, he is often praised for his use of this language because it is considered an indication of vernacular speech, or dialect, which is a speech pattern specific to a region or group of people. Some scholars

9

argue that Mark Twain's greatest gift was his ability to use vernacular speech effectively. For example, Shelley Fisher Fishkin, in her groundbreaking book *Was Huck Black? Mark Twain and African-American Voices*, writes: "Mark Twain was unusually attuned to the nuances of cadence, rhythm, syntax, and diction that distinguish one language or dialect from another, and he had a genius for transferring the oral into print."[4]

Furthermore, though there are still some objections to the portrayal of characters with seemingly low moral standards, these objections are significantly overruled by a much more sensitive subject: racism.

2000: Enid, Oklahoma

The issue of racism caused a furor in Enid, Oklahoma, in 2000. Enid is a large town of about fifty thousand, and *Adventures of Huckleberry Finn* had been required reading for high school juniors for many years.[5] In November 1999, a group of African-American ministers who were members of a coalition called the Southern Heights Ministerial Alliance submitted an official complaint to the school district. They argued that the novel's language was offensive to black students, especially because of the use of the word *nigger*, which appears in the novel more than two hundred times. One of the ministers said that the term eroded "the dignity, respect and self-esteem" of African-American students.[6] The group felt that "no matter when the book was written, the word is still offensive, and no matter

10

what the literary value, it is still offensive."[7] They asked that the book be removed from required reading lists, although they did not demand that the book be removed from the school library shelves. Opponents to the ministers' motion included members of the school board, who believed the novel was a useful tool for teaching American literature and history, especially the country's history of slavery and civil rights.

The debate quickly became heated, and both sides argued their opinions passionately. Soon, the discussion was not just about the use of a particular book in a particular classroom. Now it was about racism and Enid's racial history. Some participants began to bring their experiences of segregation and prejudice to the table, in addition to their views on the novel. The two sides agreed that no one wanted to harm the town's children, but they could not see eye to eye on *Huckleberry Finn*. The ministers' coalition and its supporters believed that students would be hurt if they read the book. The school board and its supporters, on the other hand, felt students would be harmed if they did not read it.

Enid's students did not take a stand as a group on one side or

Where's the "The"?

Many people believe that the real title of Mark Twain's best-known book is *The Adventures of Huckleberry Finn*. However, Twain made a point of leaving "the" out of the title, so it is properly referred to without the article.

the other. Many said that the book should remain in the classroom, but they were not too excited about the debate raging among the town's adults. Others, however, felt as strongly as those involved in the debate. Someone even put a note in the back of his car exclaiming "Save Huck Finn."[8] One student, an African-American sophomore who had read the book when she was younger, liked the book, but she did not

More than one hundred twenty years after the first publication of Adventures of Huckleberry Finn, *the debate over the novel's status on the library shelf continues.*

think that students should have to read it if they were offended. She said, "Some of the language is kind of harsh but it was an OK book…. It has a good message in it if people would look deeper than just the words…."[9] Other students, however, apparently felt very differently. Unfortunately, as the ministers' coalition argued, they did not feel that they could say anything to their peers or teachers for fear of being insulted with the very language that was causing the offense or because they were afraid they would get a lower grade. One of these students, an honors student who had graduated the year before the debate began, wrote a letter to the committee explaining her feelings.

She said that "she was hurt by the book and would like to see it removed as required reading."[10]

In an attempt to ease some of the tension, the school district contacted Jocelyn Chadwick, an assistant professor at Harvard University's Graduate School of Education. Chadwick, a leading scholar on Mark Twain, is an African American whose ancestors were slaves on both sides of her family. Her parents were active in the civil rights movement when she was young, and she says that they gave her *Adventures of Huckleberry Finn* when she was just a child.[11]

Chadwick believes that *Huckleberry Finn* should be taught to students in part because of the debates that it often sparks and because it is a significant work by one of the country's most well-known writers. She has pointed out that race is one of the most complex issues in today's society, and she recognizes that it is very difficult for people to talk about. She has said:

> Through the controversy surrounding this book alone, Twain brings into schools what all of us in this country desperately need, yet fear, most: discussions—frank discussions—about race, race relations, interracial relations, race language, racial stereotypes and profiling, and, ultimately, true and unadulterated racial equality.[12]

Chadwick recognizes that *Huckleberry Finn* is a difficult novel that deals with harsh issues, but she also believes that it is the job of a good book to make the

13

reader think. She said, "You're left with conundrums at the end of 'Huck Finn.' You're left with no answers.... Twain did not write a novel that's meant to make you feel good."[13]

Chadwick traveled to Enid, where she spoke with board of education members and many other interested people, including students, members of the ministers' alliance, and even state officials. In the end, the town asked Chadwick to return and lead a workshop for teachers about how to teach the novel appropriately in a high school classroom. The workshop—which included discussions about the book's place in history, teaching strategies, and useful resources—was a great success. Ultimately, the school board voted to keep *Adventures of Huckleberry Finn* in the curriculum, provided that teachers participate in training sessions before using the book in their classrooms.

Chapter 2

Why Ban Books?

Why would anyone want to keep someone from reading a book, watching a film, or listening to a certain kind of music? What harm could come of the act of reading, viewing, or hearing a given work, and what would anyone gain by forbidding that work? Is the prohibition of particular works of literature or art something that has only begun in recent years, during times of heightened sensitivity toward personal and cultural differences and identity, or is it something that began long ago?

What Is Book Banning?

Book banning occurs when an individual or group denies access to a given work by the general public or by a certain segment of the public—for example, students at a local junior high school. A book *challenge* happens when someone tries to remove or restrict access to a book. Often, people who try to ban books do so because they feel there is something objectionable

15

about the works, and they believe strongly that if the books are available, readers' thoughts or behaviors will be affected negatively.

Book banning is a kind of *censorship*, which is the act of controlling information or the expression of ideas. Censorship can affect what readers or viewers see in the newspaper or on television, what kind of art is displayed at museums, what someone says in a speech or writes on the Internet, and much more. Sometimes *censors*—individuals denying access to the works in question—are simply concerned community members; sometimes they are government officials. Censors may disagree with the opinions presented in a given work, or they may believe that the public should not have access to that work for a wide variety of reasons. For example, a parent may believe that a particular sculpture is obscene and therefore inappropriate for display in a public garden, or a government official may deem certain information classified for the sake of national security, or a teacher may feel that a given text is racist and that it gives students the message that racist behavior is acceptable. Censors often believe they are protecting society from serious harm; sometimes they simply want to stifle opinions different from their own.

Censorship in the Ancient World

Censorship has been in existence since the dawn of the written word. The works of some scholars were banned in ancient Greece from as early as the fifth century B.C., and there were serious consequences imposed upon

16

those who went against the government's rulings. For example, in 339 B.C., the philosopher Socrates was accused of being disrespectful of the gods and corrupting the youth of Athens through his teachings. Despite a strong defense speech, versions of which were documented by the philosophers Plato and Xenophon, Socrates was sentenced to the ultimate form of censorship—death. He was forced to drink hemlock, a powerful poison, and his death has been immortalized in art and literature as a reminder of the impact of censorship.

With such heavy consequences, it is not surprising that censorship was a hotly debated topic even then, and philosophers sometimes agreed that censorship was necessary. For example, in *The Republic*, the great Athenian philosopher Plato argued that art and literature should be controlled by censors to some degree in an effort to protect children during their education.[1]

Terms Related to Book Censorship

ban—To remove or deny access to a book or other material.

censor—To prevent the publication or dissemination of material that is considered objectionable, sensitive, or harmful.

censorship—The act of controlling information or the expression of ideas.

challenge—To file a formal protest against the inclusion of a book in a library or school curriculum.

restrict—To limit the circulation of a book to people of a particular age or those who have parental approval.

The power of censorship was not limited to Greece. Many scholars believe that Emperor Augustus banished the poet Ovid from ancient Rome in A.D. 8 because he was offended by his erotic poem *Ars Amatoria* (*The Art of Love*).[2]

In 213 B. C., on the other side of the globe, the Chinese emperor Shih Huang Ti, also known as Qin Shi Huang, had many books burned and many scholars executed in an attempt to preserve the emperor's version of history and unify the country under his rule. Although the emperor is credited for having succeeded in unifying China, many important works of literature were destroyed in the process, including much of the scholarship of the philosopher Confucius.[3]

The Church and the Middle Ages

During the Middle Ages, the Catholic Church kept a close watch on the publication of books and saw to it that only works that were in line with the Church's teachings were allowed. Writers who printed works against the Church were charged with heresy, and some were burned at the stake as punishment. With Johannes Gutenberg's invention of a printing press that used movable type in the fifteenth century, the Church became even more concerned about the publication of heretical works. In 1559, the Vatican published the *Index Librorum Prohibitorum*, or the Index of Forbidden Books, which consisted mostly of works of philosophy and theology. A version of it is still in existence today.

18

TALCOTT
LIBRARY

Why Ban Books?

It was not just the Church that tried to control what was published. Governments and individuals with power also tried to keep a tight rein on writers and printers. As Herbert N. Foerstel writes in *Banned in the U.S.A.: A Reference Guide to Book Censorship in Schools and Public Libraries:* "Once speech could be printed, it

An engraving of a printing office in Antwerp, Belgium, about 1600. The invention of the printing press transformed the way information was spread, sometimes to the alarm of Church and government authorities.

became a commodity, to be controlled and manipulated on the basis of religion, politics or profit."[4]

The Rise of Censorship in England

In the sixteenth century, King Henry VIII and Queen Elizabeth I of England both had strict rules of censorship that gave the monarchy the power to control what was printed. Printers, for instance, were required to be licensed. In the seventeenth century, the Court of the Star Chamber, which was a small court with no jury, tried printers who were suspected of publishing works criticizing King Charles I. The court's punishments against these printers—which sometimes included torture and mutilation—were particularly cruel.[5]

In a statement against the practice of Licensing Order of 1643, the poet John Milton—the author of *Paradise Lost*—wrote the *Areopagitica*, which has become one of the most well known writings against government control of literature and the arts. In this essay, Milton wrote:

> For books are not absolutely dead things, but do contain a potency of life in them to be as active as that soul was whose progeny they are; nay, they do preserve as in a vial the purest efficacy and extraction of that living intellect that bred them.... Who kills a man, kills a reasonable creature,... but he who destroys a good book, kills reason itself.[6]

20

Despite Milton's best efforts, however, the general public became more concerned with the morality of the books available. Soon, publishers and readers became the censors themselves.

One example of nongovernmental censorship is that practiced by Thomas Bowdler, an English editor who published *The Family Shakespeare* in 1818. This collection of Shakespeare's plays and poems omitted anything that Bowdler believed could not be read in front of "the family." Bowdler cut anything he considered lewd, immoral, or heretical, and he had a relatively low threshold for what he considered offensive language and behavior. For example, he changed Lady Macbeth's exclamation "Out, damned spot!" to "Out, crimson spot!" and completely eliminated the character of Doll Tearsheet, a prostitute, from *Henry IV, Part 1*. In addition to editing Shakespeare's works, Bowdler also edited parts of the Bible and numerous other books in the same fashion. The term *bowdlerize* comes from Bowdler's editing practices; it means to edit a text by removing passages considered offensive.

Censorship in the New World

Although many immigrants to the New World were trying to escape persecution from those who wanted to censor their speech and writing and prohibit them from certain religious and cultural practices, censorship was common in America in the seventeenth and eighteenth centuries. One of the most famous cases in which censorship was examined is the trial of John Peter Zenger in 1734.

John Peter Zenger was the publisher of the *New York Weekly Journal*, a humorous but intellectual weekly newspaper that published some articles criticizing the activities of New York's new colonial governor, William Cosby. Although he had not written any of the critical articles, as publisher, Zenger was responsible for the content of the newspaper. On November 17, 1734, soon after the articles were printed, Zenger was arrested on the charge of seditious libel, which is the communication of harmful statements against the government. Until this point in time, libel cases had focused on whether or not the defendant had actually printed the material in question, rather than upon whether or not something was, in fact, libelous, that is, unfairly damaging.

Instead of arguing that his client had not even published the articles in question, the famous attorney Alexander Hamilton defended Zenger by arguing that the articles were not actually libelous because the information printed in them was true. He argued that because the information was accurate, the criticism of Cosby was justified, and therefore Zenger had done nothing wrong by printing the articles. The jury decided that Zenger was not guilty for this reason, and this was the first time that the truth of the publication was used successfully to defend someone in a libel case. This argument against government censorship paved the way for future free speech cases and was one of the most important political trials in the American colonies before the American Revolution.

The Early Years of the First Amendment

After the American Revolution, the founding fathers drafted the U.S. Constitution, which is the set of fundamental laws of the United States that was ratified in 1788. Three years after the ratification of the Constitution, the states ratified the Bill of Rights, a document containing the first ten amendments to the Constitution that outlined the basic civil liberties of American citizens. The First Amendment, the main law which grants freedom of speech to people in the United States, reads:

> Congress shall make no law respecting an establishment of religion, or prohibiting the free exercise thereof; or abridging the freedom of speech, or of the press; or the right of the people peaceably to assemble, and to petition the Government for a redress of grievances.

Despite this important amendment, however, there has been debate about the limits of free speech almost since the Bill of Rights was ratified. In 1798, for example, a law known as the Sedition Act made it a crime to print or publish false or malicious statements against the federal government, its officials, or its laws. Under this law, many newspapers were shut down and their publishers were fined or imprisoned. The Sedition Act was widely unpopular, and when he became president in 1801, Thomas Jefferson pardoned many of those convicted under the law. The law's renewal was not approved in 1802.

Although the First Amendment protected Americans' right to free speech, many people were also concerned about protecting the morality of the American people. These were seen as two different but related issues. In response to this commonly held concern, Congress passed the Tariff Law of 1842, which made it difficult to import materials deemed obscene. In 1865, a law was passed that made it illegal to send obscene materials through the mail, although not everyone agreed on the definition of "obscene."

Not long after the passage of the more stringent Mail Act of 1865, Anthony Comstock began to campaign for even tougher laws against what he considered "indecent" materials. A former brigadier general in the Union Army during the American Civil War, Comstock helped to found the New York Society for the Suppression of Vice in 1873. That same year, Congress toughened the Mail Act of 1865 by passing new legislation known as the Comstock Law. Through this law, Anthony Comstock became a special agent of the post office, and in policing the mails, he held firm to the society's motto: "Morals, Not Art or Literature." As a special agent, he was allowed to arrest people who promoted what the Society for the Suppression of Vice considered indecent behavior, and as many as twenty-five hundred individuals were convicted on moral charges because of his actions.

Sometimes famous artists and their works were caught in Comstock's nets, and this occasionally caused quite an uproar. For example, in response to Comstock's attack on his work, the famous British playwright George Bernard Shaw called his actions "comstockery," which he said would become "the world's standing joke at the expense of the United States."[7]

Major Censorship Cases in the Twentieth Century

Anthony Comstock's role as moral guardian of Americans had a long-standing impact. By the start of the twentieth century, laws against obscenity had become quite strict and broad, though sometimes people still disagreed with what the censors declared as obscene.

One of the most famous debates about the nature of obscenity was over *Ulysses*, a novel by James Joyce in which readers see one day in the lives

Types of Offensive Language

- **cursing or swearing**—Using words that show hatred and/or anger, usually involving divine punishment, such as "damn" and "hell."

- **defamation**—The act of attacking or injuring the reputation of an individual by false and malicious statements. Defamation includes libel and slander.

- **libel**— A false and malicious written statement that injures a person's reputation. Similar to slander, which is spoken.

- **obscenity**—Language that is offensive to society's standards of decency.

- **pornography**—Writings, pictures, or other works intended primarily to cause sexual arousal.

- **profanity**—Irreverent speech that serves to debase what is holy, such as using names of relgious deities in a disrespectful way.

- **slander**—A false and malicious statement that is spoken aloud that injures a person's reputation. Similar to libel, which is written.

- **slur**— A term that debases a particular racial and/or ethnic group.

of two Dubliners in 1904. In *Ulysses*, Joyce experimented with many unique styles of writing, including stream of consciousness. This technique is described by M. H. Abrams as "a special mode of narration that undertakes to reproduce ... the continuous flow of a character's mental process...."[8] Through stream of consciousness, James showed characters' thoughts about everything from bodily functions to high art. Among other things, some readers found the frank and graphic descriptions expressed in stream-of-consciousness style to be obscene and, therefore, objectionable.

Ulysses had a long and arduous path to publication. Beginning in 1918, it was published serially in a New York literary magazine called *The Little Review*. In 1919, however, the U.S. Post Office confiscated copies of the magazine because it felt that portions of *Ulysses* were obscene. In 1921, *The Little Review* was found guilty of publishing obscenity. Its editors, Jane Heap and Margaret Anderson, were fined and forbidden to publish the remaining chapters of the novel. Later, Sylvia Beach, the owner of the famous Shakespeare and Company bookstore in Paris, published *Ulysses* in a limited edition in 1922, and copies of the book were smuggled into many countries that had banned the book, including England, Ireland, Australia, and the United States. Often the books passed through customs in travelers' luggage wrapped in book jackets bearing a different name; occasionally, though, books were seized by customs officials.[9]

26

Why Ban Books?

Ulysses is now considered one of the most important works of English literature, and in 1998, it was voted the greatest English-language novel in the twentieth century.[10] But in 1932, when it was sent to the American publisher Random House, customs agents seized it in New York.[11] Random House went to court to have the obscenity charge dismissed so they could legally publish an American edition of the book. At the trial, the presiding federal court judge, John Woolsey, determined that it was necessary to look at the novel as a whole and to consider how an average reader might react in order to make a fair judgment as to whether or not a work was obscene. When the judge looked at *Ulysses* in this fashion, he determined that it was not obscene, and that it was, in fact, a viable piece of art.

In his landmark decision, Judge Woolsey wrote: "In 'Ulysses,' in spite of its unusual frankness, I do not detect anywhere the leer of the sensualist. I hold, therefore, that it is not pornographic."[12] He felt that Joyce's honest stream-of-consciousness style was challenging, but that it was an important piece of artwork that did not merit a government-sanctioned ban:

> Furthermore, "Ulysses" is an amazing "tour de force" when one considers the success which has been in the main achieved with such a difficult objective as Joyce set for himself. As I have stated, "Ulysses" is not an easy book to read. It is brilliant and dull, intelligible and obscure by turns. In many places it seems to

27

me to be disgusting, but although it contains, as I have mentioned above, many words usually considered dirty, I have not found anything that I consider to be dirt for dirt's sake. Each word of the book contributes like a bit of mosaic to the detail of the picture which Joyce is seeking to construct for his readers. If one does not wish to associate with such folk as Joyce describes, that is one's own choice. In order to avoid indirect contact with them one may not wish to read "Ulysses"; that is quite understandable. But when such a real artist in words, as Joyce undoubtedly is, seeks to draw a true picture of the lower middle class in a European city, ought it to be impossible for the American public legally to see that picture?[13]

Judge Woolsey's decision was announced on December 6, 1933. Random House began printing *Ulysses* immediately. Today, many scholars consider Woolsey's decision to be a major turning point in the history of censorship laws in the United States. However, it is also important to note that by 1933, American society was starting to lessen many of the moral restrictions that had been prevalent during Anthony Comstock's time. For example, it is an interesting coincidence that the Twenty-first Amendment to the Constitution, which repealed the national prohibition of alcohol, was ratified during the same week that *Ulysses* was cleared of obscenity charges.

The necessity of taking the whole work into account when determining an obscenity charge was upheld in 1957 in the case of *Roth* v. *United States*. In this case, a bookseller was charged with sending obscene materials through the mail; in response, he argued that his First Amendment right to free speech allowed him to send the materials in question. In the end, the Supreme Court ruled that obscenities were not, in fact, protected by the First Amendment. The Court stated that in order to judge whether or not something was obscene, authorities had to take the work as a whole and to think about how the community would react to the work. Supreme Court Justice William J. Brennan, Jr., wrote that it was necessary to determine "whether to the average person, applying contemporary community standards, the dominant theme of the material taken as a whole appeals to prurient interest [characterized by inordinate interest in sex]."[14]

In 1972, the Supreme Court decided another case about obscene material being sent through the mail. This case is known as *Miller* v. *California*, and here, another man was charged with mailing obscene materials through the mail. He too felt that the charge violated his First Amendment rights and that previous rulings about the definition of "obscene" were wrong. In this case, the Supreme Court elaborated on the way to test whether something was obscene or not. The ruling stated that authorities had to determine the following when judging the obscenity of a work:

> (a) whether "the average person, applying contemporary community standards" would find that the work, taken as a whole, appeals to the prurient interest.... (b) whether the work depicts or describes, in a patently offensive way, sexual conduct specifically defined by the applicable state law; and (c) whether the work, taken as a whole, lacks serious literary, artistic, political, or scientific value.[15]

These cases helped to clear up the definition of obscenity from the point of view of the government and the American legal system. Unfortunately, it did not necessarily help ordinary citizens figure out how to deal with an objection to a given work. It was still unclear who had the right to decide what could be read and by whom. For example, even if a book was cleared of an obscenity charge, someone might still object to its presence in a local library. The American public still needed clarification about whether anyone had the right to ban the book in this situation.

Censorship and Books in the School

One of the most significant cases to address book banning was the 1982 Supreme Court case of *Board of Education, Island Trees Union Free School District* v. *Pico*. In this case, several high school students, including Steven Pico, brought a case against his school after school board members removed books from the school library that they considered "anti-American, anti-Christian, anti-Semitic, and just plain filthy."[16] The school board members said that they removed the books because they felt that it was their duty and obligation "to protect the children in our schools from this moral danger as surely as from physical and medical dangers."[17] Steven Pico and some of his schoolmates disagreed.

Steven Pico and his fellow students believed that by removing the books from the library, the board members had violated their First Amendment right to freedom of speech. The Supreme Court ruled in favor of Pico and his fellow students and said that although school boards should respect community values and safeguard the well-being of children, the First Amendment rights of students should also be respected. The Court said that students do not "shed their constitutional rights to freedom of speech or expression at the schoolhouse gate" and that school libraries are a special place for the freedom of expression.[19]

Books Challenged in the *Island Trees* Case

- **Slaughterhouse-Five**
  by Kurt Vonnegut, Jr.

- **The Naked Ape**
  by Desmond Morris

- **Down These Mean Streets**
  by Piri Thomas

- **The Best Short Stories by Negro Writers**
  edited by Langston Hughes

- **Go Ask Alice**
  anonymous

- **Laughing Boy**
  by Oliver LaFarge

- **Black Boy**
  by Richard Wright

- **A Hero Ain't Nothin' But a Sandwich**
  by Alice Childress

- **Soul on Ice**
  by Eldridge Cleaver[18]

In addition to challenging works of fiction in the school setting, one of the main targets of book censorship has been nonfiction books for young readers, including textbooks. Often, people trying to censor these books do so because they want to protect their children and the children of their community from topics or language they believe to be harmful or inappropriate for young people.

Attempts to censor textbooks in the United States began during the Civil War when divisions between the North and South crossed into the classroom. Northerners and Southerners strongly disagreed about the way some textbooks portrayed the different regions and how certain historical events were described. In an attempt to save sales, textbook publishers began to censor themselves by writing one version of the book to be sold in the South and another to be sold in the North. This practice continued long after the Civil War officially ended.[20]

Challenges to books in schools are one of the reasons publishers sometimes print adaptations of famous works of literature. There are many examples of textbooks that have been bowdlerized of questionable material and language. For example, in some textbook versions of *The Adventures of Tom Sawyer* that were published in the early 1980s, the phrase "honest injun" was replaced with simply "honest."[21] The phrase was deleted because some people thought it was racist; others thought it was inappropriate for a character in a children's textbook to swear in any way. In other instances, textbook versions of some Shakespeare plays omitted entire passages that might have caused objections by some parents or school boards. Such editing is more common than many people realize and is often caused by the pressure upon publishers to provide textbooks that will be free from censorship challenges.

Sometimes, instead of trying to ban a book altogether, a challenger may seek to have the work removed from a particular grade because he or she feels that the book is unsuitable for children in that age

Church members in Butler, Pennsylvania, burn books, CDs, and videos on a bonfire. Some people believe in destroying materials that they believe threaten the morals of society.

group. When this happens, the challenger is arguing that the book is not "age-appropriate." For example, parents or teachers may believe that a particular novel includes scenes, language, or concepts that fourth graders are too young to understand or appreciate adequately. The adults may, however, feel the books would be fine for more mature readers, and they might ask that the book be reassigned to the seventh-grade curriculum. They may also request that the library lend the book only to students of a certain age or to students who have a permission slip signed by their parents or guardians.

The suitability of a work for a particular age group is a question that asks about a reader's maturity and his or her ability to understand complex language and social issues. Therefore, just as the definition of obscenity is debated frequently, so too is the term *age-appropriate*. Given that children mature at different rates—and are taught different things by their parents at different times in their lives—it is not surprising that debates over age appropriateness can get as heated as those dealing with other issues.

Book Banning in Literature

Book challenges have sometimes sparked furious responses from challengers, defenders, and sometimes authors themselves. It has even been the subject of many books, both fictional and nonfictional, including several novels for young people.

In the 1980 novel *Maudie and Me and the Dirty Book by Betty Miles*, for example, a middle school girl gets involved in an interschool reading project. After reading a seemingly harmless book to a group of younger students, the girl finds herself swept up in a community-wide debate over the book and book challenges in general.

Nat Hentoff's *The Day They Came to Arrest the Book* (1982), on the other hand, is a fictional recounting of a challenge to *Adventures of Huckleberry Finn*, told mostly from the perspective of the school newspaper editor, Barney Roth. In this novel, the community is thrown into an uproar when some students and parents raise objections to the book, which they find racist, sexist, and immoral. Students, teachers, parents, and community leaders argue on all sides, and eventually the community reaches a resolution

The Most Frequently Challenged Books of 1990–2000

1. Scary Stories (series) by Alvin Schwartz
2. *Daddy's Roommate* by Michael Willhoite
3. *I Know Why the Caged Bird Sings* by Maya Angelou
4. *The Chocolate War* by Robert Cormier
5. *Adventures of Huckleberry Finn* by Mark Twain
6. *Of Mice and Men* by John Steinbeck
7. Harry Potter (series) by J. K. Rowling
8. *Forever* by Judy Blume
9. *Bridge to Terabithia* by Katherine Paterson
10. Alice (series) by Phyllis Reynolds Naylor[22]

after each side has had the opportunity reflect and learn from one another.

One of the most famous examples of a book that addresses the issue of book banning is Ray Bradbury's *Fahrenheit 451*. This futuristic novel was first published in 1953. The book's title refers to the temperature at which paper catches fire and burns, and in the story, firemen no longer fight to put out fires. Instead, they *set* fires to homes of people who have books in order to destroy the books and punish the readers. Book ownership is a serious crime in *Fahrenheit 451* because the society portrayed believes books can lead to thinking, which itself can lead people to disagree with one another and the government.

The main character of *Fahrenheit 451* is Guy Montag, a fireman who had long been dedicated to his job. During the course of the novel, Montag questions his work and soon becomes the target of the regime he had helped to support—the regime that tried to equalize the intellectual playing field and minimize the offense some people took to books and other writings. In doing so, the firemen thought they were helping to make everyone equal and content, as argued by Montag's superior, Captain Beatty:

> We must all be alike. Not everyone born free and equal, as the Constitution says, but everyone *made* equal. Each man the image of every other; then all are happy, for there are no mountains to make them cower, to judge

themselves against. So! A book is a loaded gun in the house next door. Burn it. Take the shot from the weapon. Breach man's mind.... And so when houses were finally fireproofed completely ... there was no longer need of firemen for the old purposes. They were given the new job, as custodians of our peace of mind, the focus of our understandable and rightful dread of being inferior: official censors, judges, and executors.[23]

According to an afterword written in 1979, Bradbury was strongly opposed to the censorship of his—or any other—works. He particularly disagreed with the bowdlerization of literature, and he refused to allow his works to be published that way. To this end, he was incensed after some students wrote to him to point out the "exquisite irony" that editors had censored *Fahrenheit 451* "bit by bit" over time without his knowledge.[24] Ultimately, the publisher reset and republished the book "with all the damns and hells back in place."[25] In concluding his essay, Bradbury argued that he would continue to fight censorship:

In sum, do not insult me with the beheadings, fingerchoppings or the lung-deflations you plan for my works. I need my head to shake or nod, my hand to wave or make into a fist, my lungs to shout or whisper with. I will not go gently onto a shelf, degutted, to become a non-book.[26]

Banned Books Week

Book challenging and banning continues to occur today. According to the American Library Association, the major reasons that books are challenged are because some people think the works:

- contain sexually explicit materials,
- use offensive language,
- are unsuited to a specific age group,
- include material that promotes occult themes,
- contain violence,
- promote homosexuality, or
- promote a specific religious viewpoint.[27]

Usually, a book is challenged because someone is concerned about that book's potential negative effect on a young person or on the community as a whole. While such concern for one's children and community should be respected, many people consider this concern to be inappropriate when the book challenger tries to impose his or her opinion on the entire community. In an effort to educate the American public about the history of book banning and the potential impact it could have on one's culture and community, several organizations joined together to create "Banned Books Week: Celebrating the Freedom to Read" in 1982. The celebration is sponsored by the American Library Association, the American Booksellers Association, the American Booksellers Foundation for Free Expression, the American Society of Journalists and Authors, the Association of American Publishers, and the National Association of College Stores, and it is endorsed by the Center for the Book of the Library of Congress.

Banned Books Week takes place each year in the last week of September. According to the American Library Association, Banned Books Week

> celebrates the freedom to choose or the freedom to express one's opinion even if that opinion might be considered unorthodox or unpopular *and* stresses the importance of ensuring the availability of those unorthodox or unpopular viewpoints to all who wish to read them.[28]

During the celebration, some schools and libraries have special activities—such as lectures, discussion panels, and readings—and posters, flyers, and lists of banned and challenged books are distributed in order to educate students and other community members about the impact of banning books.

Chapter 3

Sam Clemens and Mark Twain: One Man, Two Identities

Samuel Langhorne Clemens was born on November 30, 1835. "Mark Twain" came into being in February 1863, when Clemens adopted this pen name, or pseudonym. The phrase *mark twain* is a riverboat term for two fathoms, or twelve feet. It was used to denote the line between safe and dangerous waters, and given the often challenging nature of Twain's work, this was an apt pen name for the young writer.[1] From 1863 onward, Clemens always published his works under the name Mark Twain, who became a kind of character and alter ego to Clemens. At times, it seemed as if Clemens got lost in the Mark Twain character he had created, and a few of his friends even called him Mark. On occasion, he referred to himself that way.[2] Some scholars refer to the writer as Samuel Clemens when discussing his personal and family life and as Mark

Twain when referencing his literary career. These distinctions are maintained in this book as well.

By the time he took on his famous pseudonym, Clemens was already relatively well known in Nevada, where he wrote for a newspaper in Virginia City. When he died on April 21, 1910, Mark Twain was one of the most famous Americans in the world, celebrated in all corners of the globe by the wealthy and the humble, princes, paupers, and everyone in between.

Boyhood in Missouri

Sam Clemens was born in Florida, Missouri, the sixth of seven children of John and Jane Clemens. According to Twain, Florida was a tiny village with only two dusty streets and two stores, one of which was owned by his uncle.[3] Twain's birth had a significant impact on the town's population, as he humorously claimed in his autobiography:

> The village contained a hundred people and I increased the population by 1 per cent. It is more than many of the best men in history could have done for a town. It may not be modest in me to refer to this but it is true. There is no record of a person doing as much—not even Shakespeare. But I did it for Florida and it shows that I could have done it for any place—even London, I suppose.[4]

When he was four years old, Sam and his family moved to Hannibal, Missouri, which served as the basis

41

for the town of St. Petersburg in both *The Adventures of Tom Sawyer* and *Adventures of Huckleberry Finn*. Hannibal was also a small town, and it was located on the Mississippi River, which had a major impact on Sam from an early age.

Missouri had gained statehood in 1820, only fifteen years before Sam was born. It was a state that allowed slavery, but the form of slavery practiced in Hannibal, Missouri, was less terrifying than that of its more southern neighbors, according to Twain. Although he became an ardent supporter of civil rights for African Americans as an adult, as a child, Sam did not think there was anything wrong with slavery, in part because he did not know that society could be any other way. The acceptance of slavery was very much at odds with Clemens's humane instincts as an adult. Perhaps in an attempt to understand his childhood views, Twain later suggested that the slavery of his hometown was relatively mild:

> There was nothing about the slavery of the Hannibal region to rouse one's dozing humane instincts to activity. It was the mild domestic slavery, not the brutal plantation article. Cruelties were very rare and exceedingly and wholesomely unpopular.[5]

Although Sam's family owned only one slave and hired others from neighbors, his uncle John Quarles owned several, including a few who were very influential to Sam and his young siblings and cousins.

Of particular importance to young Sam was an older slave owned by his uncle whom the children referred to as "Uncle Dan'l," and who served as the basis for the runaway Jim in *Adventures of Huckleberry Finn*.[6]

When Sam was eleven years old, his father died suddenly of pneumonia after having been caught in an ice storm.[7] John Clemens had never been very successful in business—he had been plagued by bad luck and poor decisions—and his death left the family financially unprepared. To help support the family, Sam left school and began to work as an apprentice, or assistant, for a local newspaper.

As a newspaper apprentice, young Sam learned how to set type, a job he performed for many years. Later, he worked for his older brother Orion, who had bought the *Hannibal Journal* in 1850. Although typesetters did not usually write the stories they helped to print, Sam was a humorous storyteller from a young age, and in 1851, "A Gallant Fireman," Sam's first published story, appeared in print. This sketch, a short paragraph published without a byline, told of another young apprentice at the paper who had labored to save some equipment from a fire. The equipment had not, in fact, been in any danger, and Sam's description of the event was a funny, devilish jab at his colleague. Although it would be another year and a half before Sam printed another story, the humorous style of this early piece was a precursor of Twain's later work.[8]

Life on the Mississippi

As a young man, Sam Clemens traveled in search of work as a typesetter, which he found in St. Louis, New York City, Philadelphia, and, briefly, Cincinnati. By 1857, however, he began to feel the call of the Mississippi River, along which he had played as a boy in Hannibal. In March of that year, he became a "cub pilot," a student training to be a pilot of the steamboats that made up the major traffic on the Mississippi. Horace Bixby was his mentor, and from him, Sam learned everything he could about the ever-changing river.

Although Clemens was a steamboat pilot for only a few years, his love of the Mississippi River lasted his entire life, and the river featured in several of his major works, including, of course, his most famous river story, *Adventures of Huckleberry Finn*. In March of 1880, nearly twenty years after leaving the steamboats of the Mississippi behind, Twain received a letter from a twelve-year-old boy named David Watt "Wattie" Bowser from Texas. In his letter, Wattie asked Twain if he would be willing to trade places with him. In his reply, Twain wrote that he would be willing to return to his boyhood if he could be sure he could stay on the river. He wrote: "The main condition should be, that I should emerge from boyhood as a 'cub pilot' on a Mississippi boat, and that I should by and by become a pilot, and remain one."[9]

Clemens's career as a steamboat pilot was relatively short-lived. When the Civil War broke out in 1861, the

Mississippi River was closed to commercial traffic. Although he was not trained as a soldier and he was greatly conflicted about his identity as a Southerner and as an American, Clemens joined a group of Confederate militiamen known as the Marion Rangers. Inspired by the local enthusiasm for the South, the men marched around the countryside and practiced various exercises, but after two weeks, Clemens quit and the group disbanded. After spending a short time in St. Louis with his family, Clemens headed west in July 1861 to work again for his brother Orion, who had been appointed secretary to the governor of the Nevada Territory.

Roughing It in the West

In Nevada, Sam Clemens joined the multitudes of hopeful men prospecting, or searching, for silver, which had recently been discovered in the area. Like most of the prospectors, Clemens had no luck in his search, although he worked hard and looked in several likely areas. Life in Nevada at this time was full of unexpected challenges, which Twain later wrote about in *Roughing It*,

"Mark Twain" as Character and Brand Name

As Harvard University professor Philip Fisher explains in his essay "Mark Twain," the name came to represent something larger than life:

> The name "Mark Twain" ... is more like a brand name in a commercial world of celebrity, advertisement, and packaged products like Ivory Soap, Coca Cola, and Winchester rifles. "Mark Twain" was an enterprise that included popular travel writing, coast-to-coast lecturing, door-to-door subscription sales of his books, a publishing house, and speculations in various inventions. The name was a trademark, secured by constant public witticisms and cartoons, and stabilized by a fixed and well-known eccentric appearance.[10]

published in 1872. In order to make enough money to get by, Clemens soon returned to the newspaper world, this time as a writer, not a typesetter. He quickly became a regular contributor of news and humorous anecdotes to the *Territorial Enterprise,* a newspaper in Virginia City, Nevada. It was in this paper that he first used the name Mark Twain in 1863. By this time, the young writer was already establishing a reputation as an eccentric and humorous prankster whose bushy eyebrows and congenial manner made him stand out in any crowd. When he was around—whether known as Sam Clemens, the man, or Mark Twain, the writer—the rising star commanded attention.

In 1864, Twain went to California to work as a reporter for the San Francisco *Morning Call* and the *Sacramento Union.* A year later, his short story "The Celebrated Jumping Frog of Calaveras County" was printed in the *New York Saturday Press* and other papers across the United States. His name soon began to be recognized across the country. Newspapers began to print his stories and hire him to write travel letters from interesting and exotic places. Such letters were popular items in newspapers of the day, and since Clemens loved to travel, he was drawn to the work because it gave him the opportunity to see new places. Unfortunately, he occasionally got so involved in the thrill of his travels that he got behind on his letter-writing duties. Eventually, he caught up with his assignments, though it sometimes took a few months.

Twain's travel letters were a great success. In 1866, for example, he traveled to the Sandwich Islands, which is what Hawaii was called before it became a state. As a record of his journey, he wrote letters home to the Sacramento *Union*. Readers were enthralled. After being printed in Sacramento, the letters were published in newspapers throughout the country, which gave many people the opportunity to read his work for the first time. When Twain returned to California, he gave a

The young writer was establishing a reputation as a humorous prankster whose bushy eyebrows and congenial manner made him stand out in any crowd.

series of popular lectures about his adventures, an enterprise he would repeat many times in the future.

Although he had only just returned to California from his Pacific travels, Clemens was not ready to settle down, and he soon decided to embark on another exciting trip. This time, he was hired by the *Alta California* to travel to the East Coast, where he lived for a time in New York City. He then decided to join a group of tourists traveling aboard a boat called the *Quaker City* to Europe and then to the Middle East, or what the tourists referred to as the Holy Land. With their plans to visit Jerusalem and other sites in Christian history, the *Quaker City* travelers were mostly religious Christians, and the young Mark Twain was a rough and tumble exception to their pious group. The journey had a great impact on Twain, and he later turned his *Alta California* letters into his first book, *The Innocents Abroad*, which was published in 1869.

Twain's trip on the *Quaker City* was a significant career move, but it also had a major impact on his personal life: He met his future brother-in-law, Charles Langdon, the brother of Olivia Langdon.

The Langdon Family

Jervis Langdon was born in 1809 and married Olivia Lewis in 1832. A storekeeper turned businessman, Langdon was an intelligent, hardworking man who came to own a successful lumber and coal business in Elmira, a thriving city in the south central part of New York State. In his biography of Mark Twain, Justin Kaplan described the Langdons as "mainstays of church and community" who used their wealth "with liberality and without ostentation."[11] Staunch abolitionists, or people who believed that slavery should be abolished, the Langdons helped slaves to escape to freedom along the Underground Railroad, and they were friends and regular hosts of such African-American leaders as Frederick Douglass. The Langdons were serious, principled people who supported women's right to vote, the temperance movement (which recommended the avoidance of alcohol), and several other reform campaigns.[12]

Jervis and Olivia Langdon had three children: an adopted daughter, Susan Dean, born in 1836; a daughter,

Olivia, or Livy, born in 1845; and a son, Charles, or Charley, born in 1849. The children were well-educated and raised with their parents' values. Livy was especially interested in her studies, and she and her parents believed strongly in the positive impact of education on women, still a relatively rare belief at the time. Unfortunately, when she was sixteen, Livy became ill with a strange malady that left her housebound and partially paralyzed for nearly six years.[13] After recovering from the illness, she remained in fragile health for the rest of her life.

Sam Clemens met Charley Langdon on the voyage to Europe and Jerusalem with the travelers from the *Quaker City*. The Langdons had sent Charley, age seventeen, on the journey in hopes that the generally religious group would have a positive, sobering influence on their son. The rough-hewn writer from Missouri was probably the last person with whom they wanted him to associate, but Charley was drawn to Clemens, who already had notoriety as the boisterous Mark Twain. On the voyage, Charley supposedly showed Clemens a miniature ivory portrait of his sister Livy, and Clemens claimed that he fell in love at first sight.[14]

Although Livy was known to be rather quiet, once he came to know her, Clemens believed her to be full of passion and energy. Decades after their first meeting, he described her in his autobiography as if still awe-struck with love. He wrote, "Under a grave and gentle exterior burned inextinguishable fires of sympathy, energy, devotion, enthusiasm and absolutely limitless affection."[15]

Clemens met Livy soon after returning from the *Quaker City* voyage, but it would be another two years before they were married, in February 1870. After the marriage ceremony in Elmira, New York, the couple traveled to Buffalo, where they intended to live in an inexpensive boardinghouse while Clemens worked as the part owner and editor of a daily newspaper, the *Buffalo Express*. Upon their arrival in Buffalo, however, Sam and Livy Clemens were surprised to find that Livy's father had bought them a beautiful house and filled it with lovely furnishings and helpful servants. The newlyweds were shocked at first by the gift, but they soon settled in gratefully.

Unfortunately, while the couple was happy in their marriage, there were tough times ahead. In August, Livy's father, Jervis, died after a long illness, and a month later, Livy's childhood friend, Emma Nye, died while visiting Livy, who was several months pregnant. The remainder of her pregnancy was challenging, and in November, Livy gave birth to a baby boy who arrived a month early. Sam and Livy named the baby Langdon in honor of his grandfather. Sadly, mother and child were dangerously ill after the delivery, and both barely made it to the New Year.

In 1871, in an effort to put Buffalo—with its difficult memories and cold winter—behind them, the Clemens family moved to Hartford, Connecticut, a hotbed of progressive writers and intellectuals, where both Livy and Sam had connections. In Hartford, Sam Clemens was near his publisher, Elisha Bliss of the American Publishing Company, and he was able to develop his association with several of Hartford's most famous citizens, including his neighbor, the writer Harriet Beecher Stowe; her half-brother, the influential minister Reverend Henry Ward Beecher; and Joseph Twichell, a local minister with whom he became particularly close friends. Within a year of moving to Hartford, *Roughing It*, the memoir of his days prospecting for silver in the Southwest, was published.

Although Livy still had not regained all of her strength, she became pregnant again in the summer of 1871. She gave birth to a daughter, Olivia Susan, known as Susy, in March 1872. Unfortunately, although Susy was doing well, the hard times of Buffalo had followed the Clemens family to Hartford. Baby Langdon's health deteriorated later that spring, and he died of diphtheria in June.

The Clemenses were devastated by Langdon's death, but friends and family helped them through their grief. Fortunately, baby Susy was bright and healthy, and soon Livy became pregnant again. The couple's second daughter, Clara Langdon, was born in 1874, and their youngest child, Jane Lampton, called Jean, was born in 1880.

A Family on the Move

Originally, Sam and Livy Clemens had rented a home in Hartford while they continued to travel back and forth

This photo of Twain was taken in 1867 in Constantinople (today's Istanbul, Turkey). Twain became well known for his lively travel writing.

to Elmira and elsewhere. Eventually, however, they decided to buy land and build a home, which they had designed specifically for them. Their new home, which they would finally move into in 1874, was on Farmington Avenue, and it would prove to be as eccentric as its famous owner. Justin Kaplan, one of Twain's biographers, described the huge house as "permanent polychrome and gingerbread Gothic; it was part steamboat, part medieval stronghold, and part cuckoo clock."[16] Despite its oddities—or perhaps because of them—the Clemens family called the Farmington Avenue house home for seventeen years.

Though he had a home base in Hartford, Sam Clemens's wanderlust did not allow him to ever remain at home for very long. In an effort to earn some money to help pay for the ever-increasing expenses of building their new home, Twain continued to lecture throughout the United States, and in the fall of 1872, he traveled to England for the first time. At that time, living in Europe was inexpensive compared to living in the northeastern United States. Thus, in an attempt to save money, the Clemens family regularly traveled abroad.

Much of Twain's work of the 1870s and 1880s was written in Hartford and in Elmira, where the rest of the Langdon family still lived. The Clemens branch of the family was particularly close to Livy's siblings, especially Susan Dean, who had married Theodore Crane, a former office manager and head clerk for Jervis Langdon. The Cranes lived in a lovely house overlooking Elmira. The house, which had been left to them by

53

Livy's father, was known as Quarry Farm in reference to an abandoned quarry nearby. Near the house, the Cranes built a small writing studio for their famous brother-in-law to work in when he and his family came to visit, which was often. This was a small wooden house with eight sides, each with a window looking out over the beautiful countryside. When staying with the Cranes in the summertime, Twain would spend most of the day in this studio writing at a small table. According to Fred Kaplan, this studio was a writer's heaven:

> With a modest fireplace, a peaked roof, vine-covered outer walls, and a window in each of its eight sides, the study had a commanding view down the hill to Elmira and the river a few miles to the west, and to the tree-covered hills of southern New York State and northern Pennsylvania in the distance. It was to become his summer paradise, the place in which he would create much of his best and best-known writing.[17]

Twain frequently consulted Livy about his major writing and lecture plans. He also shared drafts of his works with fellow writer William Dean Howells. A respected author and critic, Howells was the editor of the influential literary magazine *Atlantic Monthly* from 1871 to 1881. After their meeting in 1869, he and Twain became lifelong friends. Livy and Howells were Twain's main editors, and he relied on them heavily. According to Fred Kaplan, "Livy acted as his shield mostly on moral matters, Howells on stylistic."[18] The opinions of both were essential to Twain, as each embodied important characteristics of his audience— Livy represented the general reader, Howells the intellectual—and neither could be ignored.

Chasing the Financial Dream

From an early age, Sam Clemens always worried about money, perhaps because of the strained finances of his family as a child. Prospecting for silver and investing in new inventions, including some of his own, were failures, but defeat did not stop Clemens from trying again and again. When he married Livy, Clemens seemed to have fewer financial worries because she came from such a wealthy family. Regardless, he was immediately concerned that he would not be able to support his wife in the fashion to which she was accustomed.

Upon the death of her father, Livy inherited a significant fortune, but neither she nor her husband was particularly adept at managing it. To make matters worse, Clemens often entered into business partnerships that suffered from everything from bad luck to poor planning. For example, he eagerly invested in a typesetting machine known as the Paige compositor, which was a financial failure because it was totally impractical to produce on any marketable scale. In another poor business move, Clemens set up his nephew by marriage, Charles Webster, as a book publisher. Though C. L. Webster and Company published some of Twain's most popular works, including *Adventures of Huckleberry Finn*, the company's only other successful business venture was the publication of the memoirs of Ulysses S. Grant, which came out in 1885. By 1891, the Clemens family was in so much debt that they had to leave Hartford for Europe, where they could live on a smaller budget.

According to Twain's autobiography, the 1890s were a tough time for the family because of their debt and their self-imposed exile. Livy, however, was determined that they would make it through their trials—and repay every penny they owed. For this, Clemens's love for her rose even further:

> [Livy] was always cheerful; and she was always able to communicate her cheerfulness to others. During the nine years that we spent in poverty and debt she was always able to reason me out of my despairs and find a bright side to the clouds and make me see it. In all that time I never knew her to utter a word of regret concerning our altered circumstances, nor did I ever know her children to do the like. For she had taught them and they drew their fortitude from her. The love which she bestowed upon those whom she loved took the form of worship, and in that form it was returned—returned by relatives, friends and the servants of her household.[19]

In 1894, Sam Clemens was forced to declare bankruptcy when C. L. Webster and Company went

Challenges Beyond *Huck* and *Tom*

Most people know about the frequent challenges to *Adventures of Huckleberry Finn* and *The Adventures of Tom Sawyer*. Such challenges are often in the news, and both books are regularly discussed during annual Banned Books Week events. They are not the only writings of Mark Twain that have been challenged, however. In 1906, for example, Twain's novel *Eve's Diary* was banned from a library in Charlton, Massachusetts, when librarians objected to a picture of Eve dressed in "Garden of Eden" style, or partially nude.[20]

Furthermore, many of Twain's writings from later in life were so significantly changed during the editorial process that some scholars argue that the resulting publications were censored, not merely edited. Critics of these actions argue that the censored versions dampen the impact of Twain's criticism of what he considered the government's imperialistic activities and society's general racist tendencies. This, in turn, has made it difficult for readers to truly understand the complexities of Mark Twain as a humorous writer *and* social critic. The scholar Jim Zwick, for example, suggests that the uncensored/unedited version of "The United States of Lyncherdom," an essay that Twain wrote in 1901, would help students understand Twain's stance on race relations in the United States:

> As Twain wrote it, the essay is a stronger and more precisely targeted denunciation of racial violence in the United States than the censored version originally published in 1923. As Twain's last major writing on race relations in the United States, the essay is fundamentally important for understanding his views on race and his major novels on the subject, *Huckleberry Finn* and *The Tragedy of Pudd'nhead Wilson*.[21]

under. In an effort to pay back his debts, he went on a worldwide lecture tour, the only surefire way he knew to earn money. Livy and their daughter Clara accompanied him on his trip, which included travels to India, Australia, New Zealand, and South Africa, among many other countries. Before the tour began, he planned out three different programs so that he would not have to repeat himself before every audience. He told stories that audiences knew—like *Huckleberry Finn* and "The Celebrated Jumping Frog of Calaveras County"—and shared new anecdotes and observations in turn. As described by scholar Fred Kaplan, he was welcomed around the world: "His deadpan delivery, his idiosyncratic version of Missouri drawl, the slowness of his speech, the exoticism of his colloquial 'at home' performances, delighted audiences...."[22] In addition to giving Twain the chance to perform before new audiences, the trip was also a revelation to the Clemens family, who learned much about different cultures during their journey of a year and a half.

Twain's lecture tour finally ended in England in 1896, and the travelers were eager to meet up with Susy and Jean, who had been staying in Hartford during the trip. Unfortunately, just as Susy and Jean were about to set sail to meet their parents and sister in England, Susy, age twenty-four, became violently ill, and she died suddenly of spinal meningitis. Her family was heartbroken. Worse, Clemens blamed himself for her death, believing that if he had not forced his family into debt and exile, Susy would not have become ill. Following

This cartoon of Twain entertaining an audience appeared in the magazine *Puck* in 1885. Twain was famed around the world as a lecturer and humorous storyteller.

Susy's death, the Clemens family never returned to their grandiose home in Hartford, and they eventually sold the house. Their self-imposed exile continued until 1900, when they returned to the United States and established themselves in New York City.

The Final Decade

The Clemenses never fully recovered from Susy's death, and Sam and Livy mourned her for the rest of their lives. Livy, whose health was never very strong, weakened even further after the family returned to the United States, and she became seriously ill in 1903. In an effort to provide her with a better climate, the family returned to Europe, where they rented a villa in Florence, Italy. Sadly, nothing could stop Livy's deterioration, and she died in June 1904 at the age of fifty-eight.

After Livy's death, Clemens and his surviving daughters, Clara and Jean, returned to the United States, where they again lived in New York. Although he continued to travel frequently, Clemens bought a new house, called Stormfield, in Redding, Connecticut, in 1908. In 1909, the family celebrated the marriage of Clara to the Russian musician Ossip Gabrilowitsch, a longtime suitor. This happiness, however, was cut short. After having lived with epilepsy for many years, Jean Clemens suffered a seizure while in the bath at Stormfield and died on Christmas Eve, 1909.[23]

In the last decade of his life, Twain's humor turned even darker than that of his early writings. After returning to New York City after his travels, Clemens began to speak out more pointedly against the cruelty and greed he felt was prevalent in the human race, and what he saw as America's unjust imperialism. Because of their controversial nature, several of Twain's works were not published until long after his death.

Sam Clemens, also known as Mark Twain, died on April 21, 1910, at the age of seventy-four at his home at Stormfield in Redding, Connecticut. Two days later, thousands paid him tribute at a funeral held at the Brick Presbyterian Church in Manhattan, and he was buried in Elmira near Livy and their children.[24] The nation—and the world—grieved for the man who had made them laugh with a satirical and self-deprecating humor that made them question the status quo. Nearly a century later, Mark Twain continues to be recognized as one of the most important writers in American history, and his identity as a writer and ambassador for the American people is celebrated throughout the world.

Chapter 4

The Adventures of Tom Sawyer

The Adventures of Tom Sawyer tells the tale of a young boy growing up in St. Petersburg, a small Mississippi River hamlet similar to the town of Hannibal, Missouri, where Samuel Clemens spent most of his childhood. Many of the people and activities described in the novel are based on Clemens's own experiences, and though it is fiction, the novel is thought to be a relatively realistic portrait of life in a small slave-holding riverside community before the Civil War.

The Story

> "Tom!"
> No answer.
> "Tom!"
> No answer.
>
> "What's wrong with that boy, I wonder? You TOM!"[1]

The Adventures of Tom Sawyer opens with Aunt Polly repeatedly calling for her nephew Tom, a mischievous boy whom she is raising along with his ever-polite half brother, Sid, and his pious cousin Mary. Once she finds him, the reader immediately realizes that while Aunt Polly tries to act sternly toward her wayward nephew, she truly loves him dearly, and her punishments are not actually very harsh. Tom often takes advantage of his aunt's benevolence, but he loves her as well. From the beginning, the reader is led to believe that though he has a talent for getting into trouble, Tom has a good heart.

Most of *The Adventures of Tom Sawyer* centers on the daily life of the citizens of St. Petersburg and the adventures of Tom and his companions, including his school friends Joe Harper and Ben Rogers; Huckleberry Finn, the son of the town drunkard; and pretty Becky Thatcher, with whom Tom falls in love early in the novel. In the story, Tom reluctantly attends school and church—and plays hooky from both—and experiences the ups and downs of young love.

Tom has immeasurable charm and easily commands respect among the children of the town, despite—or perhaps because of—his tendency to get into trouble with the adults. He is clever, too, and though perhaps unaware of his talents, he is able to understand how children think—and how he can use this to his benefit. A famous example of his sway over the other children of the town can be found early in the novel when Tom has to whitewash his aunt's fence. It is a tedious job that Tom dreads doing, especially since the weather is beautiful and the fence to be painted seems like the biggest fence in the world:

> He surveyed the fence, and all gladness left him and a deep melancholy settled down upon his spirit. Thirty yards of board fence nine feet high. Life to him seemed hollow, and existence but a burden. Sighing he dipped his brush and passed it along the topmost plank; repeated the operation; did it again; compared the insignificant whitewashed streak with the far-reaching continent of unwhitewashed fence, and sat down on a tree-box discouraged.[2]

After thinking it through, Tom gets other children to do his chore by convincing them that it is fun rather than work—and that they would be lucky to have the chance to whitewash Tom's fence. When one of the "free boys" asks Tom if he actually likes whitewashing the fence, he replies eagerly: "Like it? Well, I don't see why I oughtn't to like it. Does a boy get a chance to white-wash a fence every day?"[3] He goes on to suggest that very few boys would be able to paint the fence to Aunt Polly's high artistic standards: "I reckon there ain't one boy in a thousand, maybe two thousand, that can do it the way it's got to be done."[4]

The other boy is quickly convinced and desperate to paint the fence. The new worker is thrilled and pleased with his "luck," but no one is more pleased than

Tom Sawyer shows a friend the joys of whitewashing a fence in an illustration from an early edition of *The Adventures of Tom Sawyer*.

'AIN'T THAT WORK?

Tom, who soon contrives to get out of whitewashing the fence completely:

> Tom gave up the brush with reluctance in his face, but alacrity in his heart. And while the late steamer *Big Missouri* worked and seated in the sun, the retired artist sat on a barrel in the shade close by, dangled his legs, munched his apple, and planned the slaughter of more innocents. There was no lack of material; boys happened along every little while; they came to jeer, but remained to whitewash.[5]

Soon Tom has a whole army of boys begging to do his job and giving him toys and treats in exchange for the opportunity to wield a brush. When the day began, Tom's gloomy mood was in stark contrast to the glorious summer day. By the end of the day, Tom's disposition is as cheery as the sunshine—he has had a wonderful time and come away from the experience rich in childish rewards. Furthermore, the day's episode has taught Tom a valuable lesson: that a task is only work if you are required to do it:

> He had discovered a great law of human action, without knowing it—namely, that in order to make a man or a boy covet a thing, it is only necessary to make the thing difficult to attain. If he had been a great and wise philosopher, like the writer of this book, he would now have comprehended that Work consists

of whatever a body is *obliged* to do, and that Play consists of whatever a body is not obliged to do.[6]

A boy with a vivid imagination, Tom is always keen to try new things and to live adventures like those he reads in his favorite books, which were stories filled with wrongfully exiled kings, brave knights, and generous thieves. One day after a spat with Becky, Tom decides to run away from home and live the life of a pirate. He convinces Joe Harper and Huck Finn to join him, and the three secretly set out for Jackson's Island, a small island in the middle of the Mississippi, which readers will recognize as an important landmark in the novel *Adventures of Huckleberry Finn.*

Aside from illustrating the day-to-day experiences of life in small-town Missouri, *Tom Sawyer* is also a murder-mystery-adventure story. One night, Tom and Huck go to the town graveyard to bury a dead cat in a superstitious attempt to remove a wart from Huck's hand. While there, Huck and Tom witness the murder of the town doctor by Injun Joe, a ruthless criminal. Injun Joe blames the crime on the drunken Muff Potter, who was present but had nothing to do with the murder. Potter does not think he killed the doctor, but since he was drunk, he believes Injun Joe and accepts the blame. Huck and Tom, however, know the truth, but they are so afraid of Injun Joe that they swear to keep the secret to themselves. When Muff Potter is about to be convicted of the crime and executed, however, Tom's

Games of "Pretend"

Tom Sawyer firmly believes that his games are vitally important. For example, before they leave for Jackson's Island, Tom insists that the boys follow pirate "protocol," or at least his version of it:

The mighty river lay like an ocean at rest. Tom listened a moment, but no sound disturbed the quiet. Then he gave a low, distinct whistle. It was answered from under the bluff. Tom whistled twice more; these signals were answered in the same way. Then a guarded voice said:

"Who goes there?"

"Tom Sawyer, the Black Avenger of the Spanish Main. Name your names."

"Huck Finn the Red-Handed, and Joe Harper, the Terror of the Seas." Tom had furnished these titles, from his favorite literature.

"'Tis well. Give the countersign."

Two hoarse whispers delivered the same awful word simultaneously to the brooding night:

"BLOOD!"[7]

conscience gets to him, and he reveals the truth. This infuriates the evil Injun Joe, who becomes a dangerous enemy.

Soon after the murder of the town doctor, Tom and Huck see Injun Joe find a great treasure in a haunted house they were exploring, and they overhear him say that he wants revenge against all those who had crossed him. After hearing him, the boys assume that Injun Joe is out to get them, or at least Tom, who had testified against him in court. Terrified, but still wanting to find the treasure, Tom and Huck search unsuccessfully for Injun Joe's hideout. Later, the boys learn that Injun Joe also wants revenge against the kind Widow Douglas because of the manner in which her late husband had treated him.

While seeking the treasure and trying to avoid Injun Joe, Tom continues to cause mischief whenever possible. One day on a picnic hosted by Becky

Thatcher, his shenanigans get him into life-threatening trouble after he convinces Becky to leave their companions and explore deep into the cave outside of town. Tom and Becky get completely lost, and they become very frightened, especially after the last of their candles goes out. The candle was their last view of the outside world, and Twain's description of its final moments echoes the anxieties felt by the children:

> The children fastened their eyes upon their bit of candle and watched it melt slowly and pitilessly away; saw the half inch of wick stand alone at last; saw the feeble flame rise and fall, climb the thin column of smoke, linger at its top a moment, and then—the horror of utter darkness reigned.[8]

If being lost in the dark were not bad enough, Tom discovers that there is another terror in the caves— Injun Joe has been hiding there in order to avoid the citizens of St. Petersburg. The outlook is grim for Tom and Becky.

Eventually, the two discover a new way out of the cave, and the town is overjoyed to find them safe and sound. In order to prevent others from getting lost in the cave, the adults of the town order the entrance closed off, not knowing that Injun Joe is still hiding inside. The evil Injun Joe dies after being trapped in the cave, and Tom and Huck become rich after finding his hidden treasure. The kind Widow Douglas offers to take care of Huck and give him a home and an education. The boys are heroes in their small town and start to plan their next adventure.

The novel ends on a light note with a conclusion in which the narrator suggests that the reader might see these characters again, an indication that Twain was already thinking about further developing the characters from Hannibal, Missouri:

> Most of the characters that perform in this book still live, and are prosperous and happy. Some day it may seem worth while to take up the story of the younger ones again and see what sort of men and women they turned out to be; therefore it will be wisest not to reveal any of that part of their lives at present.[9]

Writing *Tom Sawyer*

Twain had begun to think about the story of *The Adventures of Tom Sawyer* only a few days after his wedding to Livy. He later claimed that memories from his boyhood began to swarm around in his head as he pondered his lovely wife, who was asleep upstairs in their new bedroom at the time.[10] Although he had experienced a flood of memories from his childhood days in Hannibal, and he had contemplated writing about them at the time, he did not actually begin *Tom Sawyer* in earnest until 1874.

In 1874, he spent most of the spring and summer writing the novel. After writing about four hundred manuscript pages, though, he found himself saddled with a serious case of writer's block. This would happen to him on several other occasions, and he eventually learned that if he put the manuscript down for a while, he would be able to resume writing after a break—though sometimes those breaks would last for as long as two years. He later said that his writer's block was like losing an energy source:

> It was by accident that I found out that a book is pretty sure to get tired along about the middle and refuse to go on with its work until its powers and its interest should have been refreshed by a rest and its depleted stock of raw materials reinforced by lapse of time. It was when I had reached the middle of *Tom Sawyer* that I made this invaluable find. At page 400 of my manuscript the story made a sudden and determined halt and refused to proceed another step.... The reason was very simple—my tank had run dry; it was empty; the stock of materials in it was exhausted; the story could not go on without materials; it could not be wrought out of nothing.[11]

Twain did not finish *Tom Sawyer* until the next summer, but he learned from this experience that if he ever ran out of steam, all he needed to do was put the story down for a while and refill his "tank."

Originally, Twain had intended *Tom Sawyer* to be a novel for adults. In a letter to William Dean Howells in the summer of 1875, he wrote: "It is *not* a boy's book, at all. It will only be read by adults. It is only written for adults."[12] Howells and Livy Clemens, however, both felt strongly that the novel should be for children, and eventually, Twain changed his mind. In the fall of 1875, he wrote to Howells: "Mrs. Clemens decides with you that the book should issue as a book for boys, pure and simple—and so do I. It is surely the correct idea."[13]

By the time it was published in 1876, Twain firmly believed *Tom Sawyer* to be a book for young people. On the other hand, his introduction made the argument that though the novel was intended for children, adults could benefit as well:

> Although my book is intended mainly for the entertainment of boys and girls, I hope it will not be shunned by men and women on that account, for part of my plan has been to try to pleasantly remind adults of what they once were themselves, and of how they felt and thought and talked, and what queer enterprises they sometimes engaged in.[14]

In his preliminary notes for *Tom Sawyer*, Twain planned for Tom's boyhood to be only a brief part of the story. Originally, he intended to follow Tom through his adulthood, but while working on the novel, he changed his mind. Twain ended the novel with a brief conclusion, which explains why the story ended where it did. In this conclusion, the narrator states, "When one writes a novel about grown people, he knows exactly where to stop—that is, with a marriage; but when he writes of juveniles, he must stop where he best can."[15] Later, Twain did continue Tom's stories in other works, including *Tom Sawyer Abroad* and *Tom Sawyer, Detective*, but neither of these received the same acclaim as the original.

By the time it was published in 1876, Twain firmly believed Tom Sawyer to be a book for young people.

Publication and Response

The Adventures of Tom Sawyer was published in the United States by the American Publishing Company, which was run by Elisha Bliss out of Hartford, Connecticut. The novel was originally a subscription book, which meant that readers paid in advance in order to receive a copy of the book once it was printed. The novel was actually published in England before coming out in the United States, and copies of the book made their way to America, including to Canada, where the book was published in an unauthorized edition. Twain was furious that the book was pirated in this fashion and was frustrated that the American publication of the novel seemed to be inexplicably delayed. Eventually, the book came out in the summer of 1876, but, at first, sales were poor in comparison to Twain's previous books. The poor sales may have been due, in part, to the numerous illegal editions of the book that were available to the general public.[16]

The popular response to the book was largely positive. In general, children and adults alike enjoyed the book, which became one of the keystones to Twain's popularity during his life and after. Today, the book is considered one of the most popular novels in American literary history. In 1972, the U.S. Post Office even

Mark Twain called on his boyhood memories of Hannibal, Missouri, as he wrote *The Adventures of Tom Sawyer*. He originally thought of it as a book for adults.

issued a special stamp featuring an image of the fence-painting scene at the beginning of the novel.

The critical response to *Tom Sawyer* was generally positive as well, although some critics were concerned that young readers might find the mischievous Tom to be a role model.[17] A reviewer from the *British Quarterly Review* wrote: "It will have the effect of making boys think that an unscrupulous scapegrace is sure to turn out a noble man...."[18] Others felt that there was simply too much slang and poor grammar, as was expressed by a reviewer for *Athenaeum*, who generally liked the book in other ways:

> With regard to the style, of course there are plenty of slang words and racy expressions, which are quite in place in the conversations, but it is just a question whether it would not have been as well if the remainder of the book had not been written more uniformly in English.[19]

On the other hand, Twain's friend William Dean Howells published an unabashed rave review of the novel in *Atlantic Monthly* before the book was available in print in the United States. He specifically admired Twain's characters and his ability to capture the spirit of boyhood in Tom:

> The story is a wonderful study of the boy-mind, which inhabits a world quite distinct from that in which he is bodily present with

his elders, and in this lies its great charm and its universality, for boy-nature, however human nature varies, is the same everywhere.

The tale is very dramatically wrought, and the subordinate characters are treated with the same graphic force that sets Tom alive before us.[20]

Charles Dudley Warner concurred in his review of the novel for the *Hartford Daily Courant*, in which he compared *Tom Sawyer* to *The Innocents Abroad*, of which he also approved:

Tom Sawyer is in some respects an advance on anything that Mr. Clemens has before done— an advance we mean as a piece of literary work, careful in finish, and thought out more maturely. It has not the large, original force of the uncontrollable, spontaneous humor that in "The Innocents Abroad" carried an irre-pressible burst of merriment round the globe … but it has passages as exquisitely humorous as any in that book, and as a general thing it is more finely wrought. The passages we have spoken of above amply sustain this assertion; you can read them again and again with new delight, and indeed, we find it difficult not to read them every time we take up the book. They could not have been written without the spark of genius…. There is no one writing today who has a finer intuitive sense of the right word in the right place.[21]

Later, in an essay published in 1938, Edgar Lee Masters concurred with Howells and Warner and argued that *Tom Sawyer* had long been destined to become a classic:

Whatever comes to pass [*The Adventures of Tom Sawyer*] will remain a history of an old America, of boyhood in the free West, of the ramshackle village on the river. It has the quality of poetry, it has atmosphere, and poetry and atmosphere do not depend upon realism. They are the imperishable product of the poetical mind creating under favorable circumstance and in a mental period of happiness, peace, and tranquil remembrance.[22]

Chapter 5

Adventures of Huckleberry Finn

Adventures of Huckleberry Finn is considered by many to be Mark Twain's best work and an important part of America's literary history. Written in spurts over several years, it is, on the surface, another tale of a young boy like *The Adventures of Tom Sawyer*. A different reading, however, is that it is also an in-depth examination of life in the South before the Civil War and an exploration of the impact of slavery on both blacks and whites. Many people disagree on this interpretation of the novel, and the book's presence in classrooms and libraries has sparked debate from the time of its publication.

The Story

The reader will remember the ignorant, poverty-stricken boy named Huckleberry Finn from *The Adventures of Tom Sawyer*. In that novel, Huck is a secondary character who is poor, dirty, and superstitious.

In *Adventures of Huckleberry Finn*, Huck still has these characteristics, but we quickly learn several important things that can deepen our understanding of him:

- though he is uneducated, Huck is not stupid;
- though he does not think in the same fashion as Tom Sawyer, Huck has a vivid imagination that he is not afraid to use;
- though he might lie and swear on occasion, he struggles when he feels he is doing something wrong; and
- though he is often an outsider, he is a good friend.

On one level, *Huck Finn* is a companion book to *Tom Sawyer*, and the novel begins where the first story ends. Huck has been taken in by the kindly Widow Douglas, who tries to "sivilize" him, but Huck is uncomfortable in his new life, which he tried to escape. His old friend Tom helped to draw him back, and from the start, the reader sees the conflict raging inside of Huck:

> …it was rough living in the house all the time, considering how dismal regular and decent the widow was in all her ways; and so when I couldn't stand it no longer, I lit out. I got into my old rags, and my sugar-hogshead again, and was free and satisfied. But Tom Sawyer, he hunted me up and said he was going to start a band of robbers, and I might join if I would go

back to the widow and be respectable. So I went back.[1]

Huck is considered rich by many people in the village because of the money he and Tom Sawyer found in the cave after the death of Injun Joe. Despite this wealth, however, he is more comfortable wearing his run-down clothes and sleeping outdoors. Eventually, Huck gives Judge Thatcher his money so as to avoid having to give the money to his father, but the judge only takes it for safekeeping.

Soon after the novel begins, Huck leaves St. Petersburg with his father, Pap Finn, who had come into town to find him because he wanted Huck's

On one level, Huck Finn *is a companion book to* Tom Sawyer, *and the novel begins where the first story ends.*

newfound money. Pap Finn is a cruel and greedy alcoholic, and he forces Huck to go with him to his shanty in the woods near town. Although his father is brutal, Huck finds that he likes being out in the woods where he does not feel fettered by "sivilization." After his father becomes increasingly cruel, however, Huck decides to escape. To do so, he fakes his death and takes off down the river to Jackson's Island, where he finds Jim. Jim is a slave who has run away from his mistress, Miss Watson, because he fears he is about to be sold

Opening illustration in the 1885 edition of *Adventures of Huckleberry Finn*. The book is considered by many to be Twain's masterpiece.

E·W·Kemble
·1884·

and sent to New Orleans, where he knows he would be treated much more harshly than in St. Petersburg. Jim had heard that Huck had been killed, and at first he thinks that the boy is a ghost come back to haunt him. Huck convinces Jim that he is not a ghost by explaining his escape.

Together, Huck and Jim set off downriver, hoping to make it to the town of Cairo, Illinois, where the Mississippi connects with the Ohio River. From there, they intend to make their way by steamboat to the free states in the North, where Jim would be safe from slave catchers. Unfortunately, they pass Cairo in a massive fog and end up going farther south, deeper into slave states where Jim is in more and more danger of being captured and punished severely for running away.

As they travel down the river, Huck and Jim have many adventures. Huck shows his powers of imagination when he lies in order to keep the pair from getting caught and sent back to St. Petersburg. Whenever he and Jim come across other people in their travels, Huck gives a false name and makes up a different story about why they are on the river. In one example, Huck tells some men that he is riding down the river with his family who all have smallpox, a disease that was dreaded at the time. As soon as the men "guess" the family's illness, they immediately veer away from the raft—and Jim, who had been hiding there. Although he had initiated the lie, Huck was conflicted: he felt bad about having lied to the men and about not reporting Jim, a runaway slave, but he also was glad that Jim had not been caught. This conflict is just one of the effects of Huck's "pretends," which have much more real consequences than those of Tom Sawyer:

> They went off, and I got aboard the raft, feeling bad and low, because I knowed very well I had done wrong, and I see it warn't no use for me to try to learn to do right; a body that don't get *started* right when he's little, ain't got no show—when the pinch comes there ain't nothing to back him up and keep him to his work, and so he gets beat. Then I thought a minute, and says to myself, hold on;—s'pose you'd 'a' done right and give Jim up, would you felt better than what you do now? No, says I, I'd feel bad—I'd feel just the same way I do now. Well, then, says I, what's the use you learning to do right, when it's troublesome to do right and ain't no trouble to do wrong, and the wages is just the same? I was stuck. I couldn't answer that. So I reckoned I would bother no more about it, but after this always do whichever come handiest at the time.[2]

Huck's imagination is very different than that of Tom Sawyer; he often had trouble understanding Tom's games of "pretend" because, in part, he sees them as unnecessary. Huck has no trouble telling a falsehood when he must, but his "games" are played because they are essential to survival.

At one point, Huck and Jim are separated, and Huck takes refuge with the Grangerford family, while Jim, the reader learns, hides in a swamp nearby. The Grangerford family is fighting in a major feud with the neighboring Shepherdson family, and at first, Huck does not understand what a feud is. Contradicting the seriousness of the situation, one of the young Grangerford boys explains it to Huck as if it is a kind of game. Buck Grangerford, who is about the same age as Huck and with whom he has become good friends, says,

> Well … a feud is this way: A man has a quarrel with another man, and kills him; then that other man's brother kills *him*; then the other brothers, on both sides, goes for one another; then the *cousins* chip in—and by and by everybody's killed off, and there ain't no more feud. But it's kind of slow, and takes a long time."[3]

The Grangerford/Shepherdson feud had been going on for more than thirty years, and young Buck does not know the reasons for the fight. Despite the feud, however, one of the Grangerford daughters has fallen in love with one of the Shepherdsons. When the young couple elopes in a kind of *Romeo and Juliet* twist, the feud intensifies, and many people on both sides are killed, including Buck. Huck witnesses the slaughter from a hiding place and is horrified:

It made me so sick I most fell out of the tree. I ain't a-going to tell *all* that happened—it would make me sick again if I was to do that. I wished I hadn't ever come ashore that night, to see such things. I ain't ever going to get shut of them—lots of times I dream about them.[4]

After Huck is struck dumb by the horrors of the feud, the story turns back to the raft, a transition that works to highlight the inhumanities possible in society. Huck and Jim are reunited and both are very glad when they are able to return to the river:

I was powerful glad to get away from the feuds, and so was Jim to get away from the swamp. We said there warn't no home like a raft, after all. Other places do seem so cramped up and smothery, but a raft don't. You feel mighty free and easy and comfortable on a raft.[5]

After a few days of tranquility, Huck and Jim meet two petty criminals who pretend to be royalty and insist upon being called "the King" and "the Duke." They convince Huck and Jim to serve them as they go from town to town tricking people out of their money. In some ways, the pairs are similar—both lie and cheat at times—but when contrasted to Huck and Jim, the King and the Duke's actions highlight a greedy and self-serving side of society. As professor Philip Fisher notes,

Huck must be careful, or he will be pulled under by their ruses. Fisher explains:

> In his greatest work, *Huckleberry Finn*, Twain splits his outsiders into two pairs. The King and the Duke invade to plunder and con the many worlds along the river. Huck and Jim enter homes or towns because they must. To protect their freedom or their lives, they disguise themselves, lie, invent stories, and accept affection and hospitality in order to survive, while at their side, the King and the Duke duplicate their every ploy in the interest of hard cash.... Huck's greatest danger in the novel is that he will be contaminated by those characters whose acts parallel, while differing in subtle ways from, his own.[6]

In the end, the Duke and the King turn Jim in for a reward and then unsuccessfully try to escape from an angry mob of duped townspeople. After learning of the con men's trickery, Huck discovers that Jim is being held at a farm, which happens to be owned by the aunt and uncle of Tom Sawyer. In order to get near Jim, Huck pretends to be Tom Sawyer. He does not know that Tom Sawyer himself is on his way to visit this same aunt and uncle, and so when Tom arrives, Huck is startled—but no more so than Tom, who believes that his friend was killed weeks earlier along the river near St. Petersburg. Like Jim, Tom starts out thinking that Huck is a ghost. Huck describes their meeting on the road:

[Tom's] mouth opened up like a trunk, and staid so; and he swallowed two or three times like a person that's got a dry throat, and then says:

"I hain't ever done you no harm. You know that. So then, what you want to come back and ha'nt *me* for?"

I says:

"I hain't come back—I hain't been *gone*."

When he heard my voice, it righted him up some, but he warn't quite satisfied yet. He says:

"Don't you play nothing on me, because I wouldn't on you. Honest injun, now, you ain't a ghost?"

"Honest injun, I ain't," I says.[7]

In an effort to free Jim with Tom's help, Huck continues to pretend to be Tom, while Tom pretends to be his own brother, Sid. The ever-imaginative Tom wants to play games of pretend with his long-lost friend, and he contrives many fantastical maneuvers by which the two boys can free Jim from his captors. All of this is unnecessary, however, because Jim had actually been freed by Miss Watson, who has recently died. Tom knows this all along, but he does not reveal it until much later. Tom's hijinks culminate in an elaborate escape plan, which causes Tom to be wounded. Eventually, all of Tom's boyish games are revealed, and Jim is set free. When contrasted to the very serious—and life-threatening—danger of Jim's situation, the elaborate games show Tom's immaturity in contrast to Huck. On a broader level, they can also be read as a statement about the plight of African Americans in the time that the book was published: Though they were ostensibly free from slavery, society was endeavoring to re-enslave them by chipping away at their civil rights.

As the novel comes to its conclusion, Huck learns that his cruel father has died, so he no longer has to worry about escaping his violent tirades or keeping his money safe from his drunken binges. Tom's Aunt Sally proposes to adopt Huck and "sivilize" him like the Widow Douglas had tried to do, but Huck famously determines that he'd rather "light out for the Territory ahead of the rest" in order to avoid that fate.[8]

Huck's Moral Crisis

Though he has been taught that it is wrong to harbor a runaway slave, Huck swears to himself that he will not turn Jim into the authorities: "Honest *injun* I will [not tell on Jim]. People will call me a low down Abolitionist and despise me for keeping mum—but that don't make no difference. I ain't a-going to tell...."[9]

Later in the novel, Huck tries again to convince himself to give up Jim, believing that he is morally wrong for not doing so. He attempts to pray, but he knows that he is being a hypocrite. After much anguish,

88

Huck finally accepts that he cannot give up Jim. He says, "All right, then, I'll *go* to hell."[10] This is a major decision for Huck who, though he may not go to church, fervently believes in the concepts of eternal damnation adhered to by the society in which he lived. Many scholars see this passage as a turning point in Huck's development, especially since making such a statement against society required much bravery and commitment. On the other hand, scholars often disagree about how this development affects the novel's overall message with regard to slavery.

This apparent crisis of conscience is one of the major conflicts of the novel—and, in turn, one of the major conflicts the reader must examine. This crisis is one of the novel's most challenging issues: How can a person determine what is "right" when culture dictates his or her behavior? Furthermore, is this "crisis" of conscience a valid argument for keeping *Huckleberry Finn* in a curriculum as a tool for examining the history of slavery and racism in the United States?

More than sixty years after the publication of *Huckleberry Finn*, the literary critic Lionel Trilling argued that this crisis is a vital point in favor of the novel's greatness:

> In point of fact *Huckleberry Finn* is indeed a subversive book—no one who reads thoughtfully the dialect of Huck's great moral crisis [about aiding Jim in his escape] will ever again be wholly able to accept without some

89

question and some irony the assumptions of the respectable morality by which he lives, nor will ever again be certain that what he considers the clear dictates of moral reason are not merely the engrained customary beliefs of his time and place.[11]

Other critics disagree. Jonathan Arac, for example, is a scholar who has written a book called *Huckleberry Finn As Idol and Target: The Functions of Criticism in Our Time*, in which he argues that the debates about *Huckleberry Finn* need to be reexamined. In contrast to Trilling, Arac believes that *Huckleberry Finn* is not a subversive book at all. He writes: "Lionel Trilling praised *Huckleberry Finn* for being a 'subversive book,' ... but it seems to me that *Huckleberry Finn* is currently being read and publicly used in support of complacency [about racism]."[12] He goes on to remind readers that by the time Twain wrote *Huckleberry Finn*, slavery was already abolished, and thus, Huck's moral "crisis" has little bearing:

> Only the universally shared assumption by readers that slavery is morally unacceptable defines the moral significance of Huck's decision to go to hell; all readers recognize that Huck will not go to hell because, contrary to his society's beliefs, he is doing the right thing. But where does the book stand on racism as opposed to slavery? Here many readers have disagreed, and yet here is the crux of the pain

for contemporary black readers. If Huck has such moral insight that he is willing to go to hell for Jim's sake, why does he not find new ways of saying his new sense of the world? Why not stop using a word ["nigger"] that is part of the system he is, we suppose, rejecting?[13]

Tom Sawyer vs. Huck Finn

On the surface, *The Adventures of Tom Sawyer* and *Adventures of Huckleberry Finn* are two books for young people that share major characters. However, the novels are, in fact, very different.

Huck Finn begins where *Tom Sawyer* leaves off in St. Petersburg, which is based on Mark Twain's hometown of Hannibal, Missouri. According to scholar Fred Kaplan, though these are the novels that present the same town on the surface, "Mark Twain's *Tom Sawyer* presents the bright side of that Missouri town. *Huckleberry Finn* contains some of its shadows, particularly slavery and Pap Finn."[14] In addition to showing a darker side of St. Petersburg in *Huck Finn*, the novel also illuminates a darker side of American society in general as Huck abandons the relative sanctuary of St. Petersburg and heads down the Mississippi River.

The two novels also differ because of the prevalence of slavery in each: Slavery is discussed throughout *Huckleberry Finn*, while it is mentioned only in passing in *Tom Sawyer*. As scholar Forrest G. Robinson points

Huck and Jim on the raft. To many, the character of Jim, the runaway slave, is the most controversial aspect of the novel.

out, "That difference is an important key to the dramatic contrast in the tone and meaning of the two books."[15]

The novels also differ in terms of the goals of the main characters. Whereas Tom is most concerned with boyish pranks, being famous, and getting rich, Huck is more concerned with avoiding the chains of "society." As Professor Fisher comments on the novels' conclusions, "*Tom Sawyer* ends with boys made rich; *Huckleberry Finn* with men made free."[16]

Even the boys are portrayed differently in each novel. In *Tom Sawyer*, Tom is an imaginative boy-hero, and Huck is seen only as an ignorant, superstitious outcast. In *Huckleberry Finn*, Tom is still imaginative, and Huck is still superstitious, but these traits are painted against very different landscapes and through very different voices.

In *Huckleberry Finn*, Tom's imagination seems immature and inconsiderate, even cruel. This is especially true in the closing chapters of the novel, where Tom insists that the boys engage in elaborate games in order to free Jim, who Tom knows is actually free already. The reader also learns that though Huck has had a limited education, he is very clever and his superstitions are based on long-held beliefs. The reader "hears" Huck as he tries to make up his mind when faced with a difficult decision, and the reader feels as if he or she is able to gain entry into Huck's thoughts.

93

The Use of Dialect in *Huckleberry Finn*

In the prologue to *Huckleberry Finn*, Twain includes an "Explanatory Notice" that states:

> In this book a number of dialects are used.…
> The shadings have not been done in a
> haphazard fashion, or by guess-work; but
> painstakingly, and with the trustworthy guid-
> ance and support of personal familiarity with
> these several forms of speech.

> I make this explanation for the reason that
> without it many readers would suppose that
> all these characters were trying to talk alike
> and not succeeding.[17]

This use of vernacular speech is one of the major reasons that *Huck Finn* is both celebrated and challenged because readers have disagreed as to the validity and impact of vernacular speech. For example, when the book was first published, many readers found the language to be coarse and vulgar. Now, Twain's use of the vernacular is often praised as innovative, though still sometimes troubling. In her work *Was Huck Black? Mark Twain and African-American Voices*, Shelley Fisher Fishkin suggests that Twain's use of vernacular speech in *Huck Finn* was groundbreaking:

> Innumerable other writers since at least the
> 1830s had made vernacular speakers, white
> and black, the focal points of their fiction. But

Twain's novel was different. What was so offensive about *Huckleberry Finn*, and what helped destine it to outdistance all of the productions of his peers and precursors in the immortality sweepstakes, were one and the same thing: by making Huck the "author" of his own book, Twain validated the *authority* of vernacular culture more boldly than any book that had gone before.[18]

Writing *Huckleberry Finn*

Mark Twain wrote *Adventures of Huckleberry Finn* over the course of several years, from 1876 to 1884, and he wrote and published seven books during that time period.[19] He would begin to work on the book, write several chapters in a steady fashion, and then come to a halt for months, if not years, before beginning again. As with *The Adventures of Tom Sawyer*, this system of writing and then "recharging" did not bother him. There is no actual break in the narrative that indicates that the author had left his characters afloat for any significant time before returning to them again.

Twain surely did not realize that he was writing the novel that many would come to consider his masterpiece. When writing to his friend William Dean Howells near the start of the project, Twain wrote:

> Began another boy's book—more to be at work than anything else. I have written 400 pages on it—therefore it is very nearly half

done. It is Huck Finn's Autobiography. I like it only tolerably well, as far as I have got, and may possibly pigeonhole or burn the [manuscript] when it is done.[20]

Thankfully, he only pigeonholed the book, or set it aside for periods of time, before renewing his progress.

Publication and Response

When the novel was finally finished, it was published in 1885 by C. L. Webster and Company, which was run by Charles Webster, Twain's nephew by marriage. It was marketed as the sequel to *The Adventures of Tom Sawyer*; the book's cover page even made mention of the books' relationship by indicating that the novel's full title was *Adventures of Huckleberry Finn (Tom Sawyer's Comrade)*.

The novel begins with a reminder of *Tom Sawyer*, which received a positive audience and critical response: "You don't know about me, without you have read a book by the name of 'The Adventures of Tom Sawyer,' but that ain't no matter. That book was made by Mr. Mark Twain, and he told the truth, mainly."[21] Huck's words imply that readers are encouraged to believe his story is true. At the same time, however, this statement also reminds the reader that he or she is reading a work of fiction and that Huck is a fictional character. In recognizing this, the reader may come to realize that Huck is perhaps no more trustworthy than his creator, Mark Twain, who was also a kind of character created by Samuel Clemens.

The publication of *Huckleberry Finn* was a challenge, and the book was delayed repeatedly. As Justin Kaplan later wrote in his biography of Mark Twain, it may have seemed like a nightmare to the author:

> In time *Huckleberry Finn* would be read in ten million copies printed in nearly every tongue, and nobody would question its rank as literature. But during the winter and spring of 1885 it seemed to promise its author-publisher a scarifying lesson in bad luck, bad planning, bad timing, entrenched orthodoxy, and public humiliation.[22]

When the book finally did come out, the popular response was mixed. From the start, the book had a powerful place at both ends of the spectrum for the general reader—it was both loved deeply and hated passionately. Some readers, expecting a book identical in style and tone to *Tom Sawyer,* were extremely dismayed.

Similarly, some of the critical reviews were extremely positive, some extremely negative. Many saw Twain's wit and use of dialect as a kind of genius. Others saw only coarse behavior and improper grammar, as was described in *The Boston Herald*: "It is pitched in but one key, and that is the key of a vulgar and abhorrent life."[23] Even Twain's former publisher, *The San Francisco*

Alta California, printed a review that said the novel was "wearisome and monotonous."[24]

Regardless of how it was received at the time of publication, *Adventures of Huckleberry Finn* continued to have its foes and its champions for decades. Even today, some critics still see its language as coarse and some consider the book to be outright racist. Others, however, agree with Lionel Trilling's famous assessment:

> One can read it at ten and then annually ever after, and each year find that it is as fresh as the year before, that it has changed only in becoming somewhat larger. To read it is like planting a tree young—each year adds a new growth ring of meaning, and the book is as little likely as the tree to become dull. So, we may imagine, an Athenian boy grew up together with the *Odyssey*. There are few other books which we can know so young and love so long.[25]

Chapter 6

The War Against Twain

Although Mark Twain is often considered to be one of the most important writers in American literature, he and his work have also been severely criticized, and he often offended his audience—sometimes intentionally. Both *The Adventures of Tom Sawyer* and *Adventures of Huckleberry Finn* have been challenged almost from the time of their publication, and both books are on the list of one hundred most challenged books, according to the American Library Association.[1]

Concord Sets the Stage for Debate

In 1885, the committee of the public library of Concord, Massachusetts, removed *Adventures of Huckleberry Finn* from the library shelves. Concord was a center for liberal thinking and transcendentalism, a philosophy which is based on the idea that individuals can understand the nature of reality by exploring their own thoughts, rather than their senses. Transcendentalists also hold that intuitive thinking can lead to the ideal spiritual existence. The town had been home to such writers and philosophers as Ralph Waldo Emerson, Nathaniel Hawthorne, Henry David Thoreau, and Amos Bronson Alcott.

In the late 1880s, the transcendentalist movement had begun to abate, but the town was still a hub for serious culture and intellectualism. As such, Mark Twain's satire was not always appreciated, especially not when it seemed to disregard respectability and proper behavior. According to one library committee member, *Huckleberry Finn* was "flippant and irreverent in its style; it deals with a series of experiences that are certainly not elevating; the whole book is of a class that is more profitable for the slums that it is for respectable people...."[2] This was harsh criticism, especially from those Clemens considered his peers.

The *Boston Globe* covered the ban in both its news stories and in its more relaxed feature writings. In the latter, it poked fun at Twain—and what it saw as a community of highbrow intellectuals—by saying, "When Mark writes another book he should think of the Concord School of Philosophy and put a little more whenceness of the hereafter among his nowness of the here."[3]

Life magazine, on the other hand, saved most of its criticism for Twain, though the writers did not seem to think too highly of Concord either:

It is a pleasure to note that the Concord Library Committee agree with *Life's* estimate of Mark Twain's "blood-curdling humor," and have banished "Huckleberry Finn" to limbo. If they will again take our advice, let them banish the School of Philosophy. Concord will then rank with other well-regulated Massachusetts towns.[4]

In addition to the newspapers, many important literary figures joined in the war against Twain after the publication of *Huckleberry Finn*. Concord resident Louisa May Alcott, author of *Little Women* and *Little Men*, wrote: "If Mr. Clemens cannot think of something better to tell our pure-minded lads and lasses … he had best stop writing for them."[5] Well known, and well loved, Alcott had significant sway over the American reading public, and her condemnation added heavily to that of the Concord library and the numerous critics who had seemingly come to life to declare their distaste of Twain's newest work.

For the most part, Mark Twain found the controversy to be amusing, and he joked that the ban would help to drive sales. In a letter to his publisher and nephew, Charles L. Webster, he wrote:

> The Committee of the Public Library of Concord, Mass., have given us a rattling tip-top puff which will go into every paper in the country. They have expelled Huck from their library as "trash and suitable only for the slums." That will sell 25,000 copies for us sure.[6]

The furor set alight in Concord continued long after the first round of fires had been extinguished, and many other libraries soon followed suit, including the public libraries of Denver and Omaha.

The Challenge Spreads and Evolves

Twenty years after the novel's initial publication, *Huckleberry Finn* continued to be pulled from school and library shelves for a variety of reasons. Soon, challengers began to focus more steadily on objections to its characters' behavior. In 1905, for example, both *Adventures of Huckleberry Finn* and *The Adventures of Tom Sawyer* were removed from the shelves of the Children's Department of the Brooklyn Public Library because the heroes of the books were thought to be providing negative role models for young readers. The community objected to the fact that the boys play hooky from school, avoid church, swear, smoke, disrespect their elders,

The famous novelist Louisa May Alcott added her voice to those condemning *Huckleberry Finn* as unfit for the young to read.

steal, lie, and much more. Some of the other characters in the books, such as the murderous Injun Joe in *Tom Sawyer* and the lying King and Duke in *Huckleberry Finn*, behave even worse. The books' challengers felt strongly that such models were wholly inappropriate for young readers.

Having learned the reason for the books' removal from the Brooklyn Public Library Children's Department, Twain wrote a letter to librarian Asa Don Dickinson, in which he argued—only half-jokingly for sure—that his novels were no more inappropriate for children than the Bible. Released only after Twain's death, the letter is laced with sarcasm, especially since Twain had made it clear—to his friends at least—that both books were intended for adults and children alike:

> I wrote *Tom Sawyer* & *Huck Finn* for adults exclusively, & it always distresses me when I find that boys & girls have been allowed access to them. The mind that becomes soiled in youth can never again be washed clean. I know this by my own experience, & to this day I cherish an unappeasable bitterness against the unfaithful guardians of my young life, who not only permitted but compelled me to read an unexpurgated Bible through before I was 15 years old. None can do that and ever draw a clean, sweet breath again this side of the grave....[7]

Twain went on to ask that if there were a copy of an uncensored Bible in the Children's Department of the Brooklyn Public Library that the librarians please remove *Tom Sawyer* and *Huck Finn* from its "questionable companionship."[8]

Despite objections to the behavior and language presented in the novels, opinions about the book began to change in the mid-twentieth century, but not completely. Some parents and community leaders continued to find Tom and Huck poor role models, and they frequently challenged the books on those grounds. In 1996, for example, when a California ninth-grader stole money from his family and flew to Hawaii, his parents blamed *The Adventures of Tom Sawyer*. His mother said, "Tom Sawyer is his hero so he thought he would venture off like [Tom Sawyer] did."[9] The morals and behavior portrayed in the novels, however, soon took a secondary place in the minds of some readers who realized that there was a much more disturbing problem with the books: racism.

Times—and Objections—Change

After the Civil War, slavery was ended, but racial injustice continued throughout the United States. At the front lines of the campaign to end this injustice was the National Association for the Advancement of Colored People (NAACP), which was founded in New York City in 1909 by a multiracial group of activists. The NAACP's mission is "to ensure the political, educational, social and economic equality of rights of all

persons and to eliminate racial hatred and racial discrimination."[10] Since its founding, NAACP members
have faced violence, discrimination, and even unfair
government policies, yet it continues to be one of the
most important and effective civil rights organizations
in the country.

By the 1950s, the civil rights movement was
gaining momentum, and more and more people were
coming together to fight against inequality. In 1954, the
landmark Supreme Court case *Brown* v. *Board of
Education* was decided, and racial segregation in schools
throughout the country was outlawed, though not
without notorious instances of violence and abuse
toward minority students. In 1955, the legendary Rosa
Parks, already an active member of the NAACP, was
fined and arrested for sitting in a section reserved for
white people on a segregated bus in Montgomery,
Alabama. Her actions sparked a major boycott of
public buses, which was organized by the Reverend Dr.
Martin Luther King, Jr., who was then a young,
unknown minister. The boycott lasted more than a year
until a Supreme Court decision outlawed segregation
on public transportation.

One of the words considered most offensive to
minorities at the time—and today—is the term *nigger*,
a demeaning slur that, for African Americans especially,
is associated with white supremacy, violence, and
racism. Originally a simple variant of the term *Negro*,
the term *nigger* had been a part of colloquial speech
in the United States for hundreds of years, though it

105

had not always had the strong negative associations that it did by the mid-twentieth century. During the 1800s, for example, the term was regularly used by people of all races. Despite the fact that it was a part of common speech, it was usually used in at least a mildly derogatory fashion. Mark Twain frequently uses the term in both *The Adventures of Tom Sawyer* and *Adventures of Huckleberry Finn*, which is one of the main reasons both books are challenged frequently.

By the 1950s, the word *nigger* was becoming a distinct reminder of the injustices faced by minorities throughout the United States. Because of the frequent appearance of the term in Mark Twain's writings, more people were finding serious problems with the use of his books in the classroom, especially *Huckleberry Finn*. Later, in 1996, forty years after the Montgomery bus boycott, Chester B. Stevens, the vice president of the African American Coalition in Piedmont Hills, California, explained the impact that the word had in the 1950s—and continues to have today—on many African Americans:

> For me, each sound of the word "nigger" rings out like the sound of rifle fire as the bullet tears through the face of Dr. King, and like the shotgun blast tearing into the back of Medgar Evers, or the threats being yelled by racist adults as they block the paths of little black children on their way to school.[11]

106

In addition to finding Twain's language racist and offensive, readers were also troubled by what they considered negative stereotypes of minorities in Twain's works, especially *Huck Finn*. In particular, readers were troubled by the runaway slave Jim, who some saw as a caricature of a figure from a minstrel show. In minstrel shows, which were introduced as a form of entertainment for white audiences in the mid-nineteenth century, white men painted their faces black and performed denigrating sketches that were humiliating to African Americans. Although he is the subject of Huck's great moral crisis, some readers feel that Jim is portrayed as simpleminded and subservient to Huck, who is only a boy, and to other characters, including the crooked King and Duke. Twain's intentions on the matter are irrelevant, according to Shelley Fisher Fishkin, who writes: "Twain's sympathy for Jim may have been genuine, but Jim's voice retains enough of minstrelsy in it to be demeaning and depressing."[12]

In 1957, the NAACP declared that Mark Twain's works contained offensive "racial slurs" and "belittling racial designations."[13] Although the group claimed that it did not submit an official request to have the book pulled from public schools in New York City, the school district nevertheless removed *Huckleberry Finn* from its approved list of textbooks for elementary and junior high schools that September. The NAACP's objections were included in news reports about the book's removal, implying that the school district had been swayed by its powerful lobby.[14]

107

Even this challenge is full of controversy, however. Forty years after the removal of the textbook version of *Huckleberry Finn* from some New York City schools, Jonathan Arac, an English professor and author, argued that the media had distorted the incident. Arac points out that though *Huckleberry Finn* was removed as a bowdlerized textbook from New York City elementary and junior high schools, it was not removed from a list of accepted novels. This ultimately meant that students would have the opportunity to read Twain's original work, rather than an adaptation.[15]

In addition to finding Twain's language racist and offensive, readers were also troubled by what they considered negative stereotypes of minorities.

Regardless of the accuracy of reports of the NAACP's involvement in the 1957 challenge to *Huckleberry Finn* in New York City, by 1964, the organization's Illinois chapter had officially protested the novel's presence in public school classrooms. This time, it was temporarily successful in having the novel removed all over the state.[16] Today, the NAACP's objections to the presence of *Huckleberry Finn* in the classroom is one of the major reasons that the book remains on the American Library Association's list of most censored works.[17]

108

Although the NAACP's objections to *Adventures of Huckleberry Finn* have given significant official weight to the arguments presented by those who request the removal of the book from classroom and library shelves, the debate also remains intensely personal and emotional. In 1981, for instance, one father raised an objection to the novel's use in a junior high school classroom in Warrington Township, Pennsylvania, after "pupils, stirred up by the numerous mentions of the word 'Nigger' in the novel, had subjected his son to abuse after school hours."[18] After debating the issue, the school district decided to move the book from the junior

During its annual convention in July 2007, the NAACP held a symbolic funeral for the "N-word." Twain's use of the term has angered and upset many readers.

high to the tenth-grade curriculum, though the book remained available in the junior high library.[19]

In 1998, Kathy Monteiro, a teacher living in Tempe, Arizona, protested the use of the novel in her daughter's high school classroom because she felt the book was racist. She brought a suit against the school district that said "the assignment of the books discriminated against black students, created a racially hostile environment and caused an increase in harassment" to African-American students.[20] Monteiro also charged that the school district was "racially insensitive" for not removing the book.[21] After confrontations with school district officials, Monteiro was arrested. Eventually, the case made its way to a U.S. district court, which held that the school was not required to remove any book as a means of reducing harassment.[22]

Defenders of the novel's place in the classroom and library have often argued that the novel can be used as a means of teaching young people about the history of slavery and racism in the United States if read "correctly." Some scholars believe that there is a place in the classroom for frank discussions about racism, but that this does not diminish the very real difficulties some people have with the novel. One such scholar is Jonathan Arac, who argues that he does not want the novel to be banned, but rather, reexamined.[23] Like many who object to the apparent glorification of *Huck Finn* in American culture, Arac is frustrated by what he sees as an inappropriate lack of respect for the opinions of

110

individuals who challenge the inclusion of *Huckleberry Finn* in the classroom. He writes:

> Why must the book be rescued from African American parents and students for their own good? Why must they be the objects of pre-emptive cultural strikes? Why is it so obvious to so many authorities that their complaints cannot be taken seriously? Why must the parents and students be told repeatedly by authorities that they are bad readers, rather than being acknowledged as voices in a genuine debate over what works against racism in the classroom?[24]

On the other hand, Shelley Fisher Fishkin suggests that *Huck Finn* should remain in the classroom, but it should be one of many texts used to explore issues of race and history. She writes:

> Jim must not be the only African-American voice from the nineteenth century that is heard in the classroom. Twain's novel must not be the only book that raises issues of American race relations. The only way to counter the demeaning experience of encountering Jim's voice is by adding others, by exposing students to the eloquence of Frederick Douglass and W.E.B. DuBois, to the "signifying" wit of Charles W. Chesnutt and Paul Laurence Dunbar, to folktales and folk

111

sermons, to the rhetorical power of Sojourner Truth, to the lucid anger of Ida B. Wells. These voices have long deserved a place in our classrooms in their own right. But our new awareness of the role of African-American voices in shaping mainstream American literary traditions gives us a new argument against those who challenge the legitimacy of their presence.[25]

Today, both *Adventures of Huckleberry Finn* and *The Adventures of Tom Sawyer* continue to spark debate among students, parents, and educators throughout the country because of their portrayals of minorities, especially African Americans, and their use of the "n-word," as it is frequently described. As in Enid, Oklahoma, the conflict often spills out of the classroom setting, touching nerves made raw from years of racial discord in communities large and small. How do these communities overcome these conflicts? And why would anyone want to teach these books in the first place?

Chapter 7

Defending *Tom Sawyer* and *Huck Finn*

Although both *The Adventures of Tom Sawyer* and *Adventures of Huckleberry Finn* have upset readers for more than a hundred years, both have also received praise from around the world. Both novels have been read by millions of children and adults. It is in large part because of their popularity that Mark Twain continues to be regarded as one of the most important writers in American literature. He is one of the most beloved of authors—and one of the most hated. With so many people fighting against his works, however, supporters of Twain have often had to be as vocal as their opposition.

Banishment Backlash

By the time *Adventures of Huckleberry Finn* was published in early 1885, Mark Twain had already become one of the most famous writers and lecturers in the

United States, despite the fact that some of his readers were uncomfortable with his satirical barbs against what they considered "proper" society.

When the committee of the public library of Concord, Massachusetts, declared its ban on *Huckleberry Finn*, audiences quickly took sides, and soon the Concord ban was being reported in newspapers across the country. Some of these so-called impartial reports clearly showed their writers' opinions. The language of the *St. Louis Post-Dispatch's* report of the ban, for instance, indicated that they disapproved of the library's actions and, by extension, Concord:

> The directors of the Concord Public Library have joined in the general scheme to advertise MARK TWAIN's new book "Huckleberry Finn". They have placed it on the *Index Expurgatorius* [index of banned books], and this will compel every citizen of Concord to read the book in order to see why the guardians of his morals prohibited it. Concord keeps up its recent reputation of being the home of speculative philosophy and of practical nonsense.[1]

Other newspapers were less subtle in their criticism of Concord, such as the *San Francisco Chronicle*, which condemned the ban: "The action of the Concord Public Library in excluding Mark Twain's new book, 'Huckleberry Finn,' on the ground that it is flippant and irreverent, is absurd."[2] The paper went on to argue that the book was much deeper than a mere children's novel, and that it is "the sharpest satire on the ante-bellum [pre–Civil War] estimate of the slave."[3]

Soon, others agreed with *Huckleberry Finn*'s early supporters, such as the writers of the *Atlanta Constitution*, which praised the novel in May 1885:

> [*Huckleberry Finn*] presents an almost artistically perfect picture of the life and character in the southwest, and it will be equally valuable to the historian and to the student of sociology. Its humor, which is genuine and never-failing, is relieved by little pathetic touches here and there that vouch for its literary value.[4]

A teenager studies in a library. Some people believe that young people need guidance about what they read, even to the point of banning controversial books.

Mark Twain and Race

The popularity of *Huckleberry Finn* and *Tom Sawyer* was soon undeniable. By the mid-twentieth century, the books had become icons of literature depicting life in the pre-Civil War South, and at first, few expressed any objection to the racially charged language or the depictions of minorities. In fact, although the book is now considered one of the most controversial nineteenth century books in terms of race, in the early years, most reviewers did not comment on the relationship between white and black characters.[5]

Twain did not shy away from writing about race and racism. His novel *The Tragedy of Pudd'nhead Wilson*, for example, is one of his most in-depth examinations of slavery and the impact it has on individuals and society. It tells the story of two men switched as infants. Both men appear to be white, but one of them has African-American ancestors. According to the laws of the time, this meant he was destined for slavery. Both babies are being cared for by a slave named Roxy, who is the mother of the light-skinned African-American infant. After Roxy switches the babies, the "legally" white baby is raised as a slave, and the "legally" black baby is raised as a free child and heir to an important man. Neither child knows his true identity, and when the switch is revealed, the men find themselves unprepared for the way society's view of them changes.

Many critics argue that *The Tragedy of Pudd'nhead Wilson* has significant flaws, especially since some people believe that it does not actually make a clear

116

statement about Twain's opinions on slavery and racism. Others suggest that the book proves that Twain believed that slavery and racism were illegitimate institutions created by a corrupt society and, furthermore, that he did not believe that one race was naturally superior to another.

Even though Twain had been brought up to believe that slavery was normal and morally correct, he became an advocate for equal rights for African

> *Though* Huckleberry Finn *is now considered highly controversial in terms of race, most early reviewers did not comment on the relationship between white and black characters.*

Americans. In his *Autobiography*, he said:

> In my schoolboy days I had no aversion to slavery. I was not aware that there was anything wrong about it. No one arraigned it in my hearing; the local papers said nothing against it; the local pulpit taught us that God approved it, that it was a holy thing and that the doubter need only look in the Bible if he wished to settle his mind—and then the texts were read aloud to us to make the matter sure....[6]

117

After learning more about the effects of slavery, however, and becoming more acquainted with the abolitionist movement and the battle to secure rights for African Americans after the Civil War, Twain began to include critiques of what he saw as a racist society in his works.

Given Twain's apparent feelings about racial equality by the time he wrote both *Tom Sawyer* and *Huckleberry Finn*, it seems as if he probably would not have minded if he stirred up a bit of controversy over the subject of racial injustice. Even by the time he had married into the Langdon family in 1870, Sam Clemens had already become a supporter of the campaign for the improved rights for African Americans. He had become acquainted with Frederick Douglass, one of the most influential figures in the abolitionist movement, and in his travel writings, Twain took great pains to show his readers how people of different races might be different but not inferior.

During the furor over the ban of *Huckleberry Finn* in Concord and elsewhere, however, readers paid little attention to the novel's depiction of interracial relations and instead focused on the characters' behavior and the novel's use of improper grammar and dialect. More than twenty years after the book's initial publication, the African-American writer and educator Booker T. Washington brought the matter to the public's attention by pointing to Twain's depiction of the runaway slave, Jim:

It is possible that the ordinary reader of this story has been so absorbed in the adventures of the two white boys ... that he did not think much about the part that "Jim" ... played in all these adventures. [But] I do not believe any one can read this story closely ... without becoming aware of the deep sympathy of the author in "Jim." In fact, before one gets through with the book, one cannot fail to observe that in some way or other the author ... has somehow succeeded in making his readers feel a genuine respect for "Jim." ... In this character Mark Twain has, perhaps unconsciously, exhibited his sympathy and interest in the masses of the Negro people.[7]

Although many people would eventually disagree with Washington's sentiment—especially the challengers to *Huckleberry Finn* who were involved with the NAACP, whose original leaders disagreed with Washington on many points—Twain himself supported Washington's work, and he probably would have concurred with this characterization.

Keeping Twain on the Shelf and in the Classroom

In the 1950s, when objections were first raised regarding racist language and derogatory depictions of African Americans in *Adventures of Huckleberry Finn* and *The Adventures of Tom Sawyer*, American society once again became divided over its opinions about the suitability of the novels, especially for young people. Some people simply did not agree with the argument that the books were racist or used racist language or stereotypes. Others were opposed to the banning of books in general. Still others believed that the books used racist language but that they could still be used effectively in the classroom. Through his Web site devoted to Mark Twain, scholar Jim Zwick asks one of the most pointed and emotionally charged questions that is raised in debates over Twain's works, especially *Huckleberry Finn*:

> Can you end racism in the United States by shielding students from language and issues that make them uncomfortable, or does it need to be directly confronted, with Mark Twain's *Huckleberry Finn* being one of the books that is most widely available for that purpose?[8]

In general, defenders of Mark Twain have argued that Twain's use of the term *nigger* and his portrayal of African Americans are opportunities for discussion in the classroom regarding the history of race relations— although most agree that the language causes many challenges for both teachers and students. In arguing to retain the books in the classroom, Twain's defenders say that the term *nigger* can help to paint a clearer picture of the time in which the books take place. They also suggest that students explore the ease with which characters use the term in order to illustrate how deeply rooted racism was in America at the time—and how the

120

problem persists today. In an essay titled "Mark Twain and Race," Shelley Fisher Fishkin summarizes the defense's argument but then points out that though there might be legitimate reasons to teach Twain's works, it still is not easy. In suggesting that there might be valid reasons for Twain's use of the term *nigger*, she also writes: "This fact does not mitigate the challenge of addressing in the classroom the pain still associated with this term—a challenge that requires that the literature classroom open itself to the history of American race relations."[9]

Despite these concerns, many writers and scholars believe that if Twain's works are put into context, the challenging language and character portrayals can actually expand readers' experiences. In her collection of essays entitled *Playing in the Dark: Whiteness and the Literary Imagination*, novelist, Nobel Prize winner—and frequent defender of banned books—Toni Morrison writes: "If we supplement our reading of *Huckleberry Finn*, expand it ... to incorporate its contestatory, combative critique of antebellum America, it seems to be another, fuller novel."[10]

In an effort to use *Huckleberry Finn* effectively in the library and the classroom, some teachers and librarians address the issue of race and the "n-word" before students even open the book. Teachers may choose to encourage students to learn about the era in which Twain wrote the novel, as well as the era in which the novel is set. Students may be encouraged to discuss the term *nigger* at the very start of a unit, and some

122

teachers ask students to decide themselves how to deal with the term in the classroom.

In addition to dealing with racially charged language, many schools are concerned with the general treatment of a controversial book. In an effort to prepare students to include a novel like *Huckleberry Finn* effectively in literature or history curriculum, some classes read articles or watch videos about the controversy surrounding the novel and discuss the history of challenges to the book as an introduction to their own studies. Other classes use the novel as a jumping-off point for discussions of book challenging in general. These classes often use their library and the Internet to research other instances of book challenging.

One popular classroom activity is the staging of a mock trial to determine whether or not the controversy surrounding *Huckleberry Finn* is valid. Through this activity, students become engaged in both sides of the argument, and proponents of this activity argue that it helps to provide an effective forum for dialogue.[11]

Chapter 8

Closing Arguments

Mark Twain's books have caused a furor since their publication, but the reasons for this furor have changed significantly over the past century. What does this uproar say about our society and how can challenging—or defending—Twain's books make a difference?

Standing Up to the Status Quo

When Samuel Clemens was a young boy growing up in Hannibal, Missouri, he was taught that slavery was both natural and right. As a naive child, he never questioned the institution of slavery because there never seemed to be the possibility of doing away with slavery within the culture of his hometown. Perhaps as a means of reconciling his early acceptance of slavery with his beliefs in racial equality in later life, Twain insisted that the slavery that existed in Hannibal was not like the slavery of the plantations that could be found in the Deep South. In suggesting this, however, he was not arguing that slavery was ever morally acceptable. Still, he suggested

124

that compared to slaves in the Deep South, Hannibal's slaves were treated kindly. Families were rarely separated and severe beatings were not common. When instances of cruelty or even murder happened, they were looked down upon by the townspeople. Nevertheless, neither he, nor Hannibal's other white citizens condemned the perpetrators of this cruelty, regardless of whether or not they approved. Within that society, people did not often question their own behavior or the status quo.[1]

When Sam Clemens grew older and he became exposed to people who questioned the validity of slavery, he began to realize that it was possible for him to disagree with the society in which he had grown up. As he traveled the world, and especially after he met the Langdon family, he began to believe that the unequal treatment of minorities and women was wrong. His books and his speeches became a platform from which he could express his opinions. Rather than lecture sternly, however, Twain used humor to engage his audience. In doing so, he was able to criticize those things he disagreed with in society while simultaneously making people laugh. While laughing, however, his readers and listeners were encouraged to think and question such issues as inequality, political corruption, religious hypocrisy, and more.

Is the Pen Mightier Than the Sword?

At first, readers of *The Adventures of Tom Sawyer* and *Adventures of Huckleberry Finn* did not react strongly to the relationships between blacks and whites in the novels. Instead, some readers were concerned that young people would try to imitate the books' protagonists. They wanted their children to grow up to use proper language, to behave politely, and to refrain from engaging in dangerous activities, and they felt that

Twain was able to criticize those things he disagreed with in society while simultaneously making people laugh.

Twain's works encouraged them to do just the opposite. In the mid-twentieth century, some people began to feel that Twain's language and his depiction of African Americans could inflict harm on readers because they felt that it stood in the way of positive growth in the countrywide efforts to move toward racial equality. Regardless of their reasons, however, by trying to stop people from reading his works, challengers have unwittingly proved that Twain was, indeed, a powerful writer whose books continue to raise issues that need to be examined by society.

A Mirror of Society: Book Challenges

In her book about book challenges and the impact these challenges can have on libraries, Emma Boardman argues that literature is a powerful way to explore challenging social issues because of the way people react to it emotionally:

126

Like the real world, fiction and nonfiction alike are full of difficult thoughts. They engage the emotions. Their explorations are far more complex than charts or figures, transcriptions of what happened, lists of moral rules, or instructions on how to act.[2]

Because it evokes an emotional response while simultaneously allowing readers to distance themselves from the issue at hand, Boardman suggests that literature can be the most effective mirror of society.

In addition, just as books are often a reflection of the society in which the author lives, so too are book challenges, which can be an illustration of the concerns within certain segments of society. Robert Cormier, the author of *I Am the Cheese* and other frequently challenged books for young people, has spoken about the impact of book banning on both writers and readers. In doing so, he recognizes that book challengers are usually trying to protect the reading public, especially children and young adults: "[Censorship is] the act of sincere, sometimes desperate people who are frightened by the world they live in and in which they are bringing up their children."[3]

Despite their desire to protect young people, Cormier argues that this goal is unrealistic and that it can, in fact, have the opposite effect in that it may keep children ignorant of the problems in the world:

[Book challengers] are trying to do the impossible, to shield their children from this world,

127

to control what they see and do, what they learn. At a moment when their children are reaching out beyond the boundaries of home and family, they are raising barriers to that reaching out. Instead of preparing them to meet that world, they want them to avert their eyes and remain in impossible exclusion.[4]

The Future for *Tom* and *Huck*

For more than a century, people have been arguing over Mark Twain's works. Just as reading the books can be an enlightening experience, an examination of the challenges themselves can also provide readers with an insight into today's society and the ways things were years ago. For example, the challenges against *The Adventures of Tom Sawyer* and *Adventures of Huckleberry Finn* that are raised on the grounds that the books promote racist behavior show a change in society's attitude about racial equality over the past century. In Mark Twain's time, the general population did not generally think about racial equality, and those people who did speak out about the issue were encouraged to keep silent. Today, racial equality is no longer such a taboo subject, but the challenges to Twain's works indicate that there are still many hurdles to overcome. As Twain scholar Jim Zwick has noted, this societal development is "an indication of increased awareness and concern about the issue in American society."[5]

128

Race relations and the issue of tolerance toward people of different backgrounds continue to be major issues in the United States. While the civil rights movement has had a significant impact on American society, prejudice against minorities is not uncommon. In addition, although tolerance and understanding are discussed more frequently in today's society, there is also much distrust of people who are new to the United States or who behave differently from the norm.

Although *Huckleberry Finn* and *Tom Sawyer* were written in the nineteenth century, some people argue that the power of the novels lies in the way they continue to allow readers a lens through which they can look at modern-day culture. Thus, it is likely that these novels will continue to cause concern among readers because of the way the characters speak, behave, and interact with one

Twain as a Teaching Tool

Scholar Jocelyn Chadwick believes that Twain's novels can be teaching tools for confronting racism. However, she recognizes that they are not a cure for the racial tensions in America. She writes:

In no way am I asserting that this novel is the ultimate answer to discussing race relations in this country or even in the English/language arts classroom. What I am asserting is that change begins, must begin, with one individual. And while that one individual who connects with someone else will not cauterize the racial chasm, the connection does create a ripple in the great racial ocean that continues concentrically. By questioning racism in his own time and provoking discussion in ours, Twain provides just such a connection for many students.[6]

129

another. Far from being offended by the novels' continued ability to cause criticism, Mark Twain would surely be impressed by the books' lasting presence in American literary culture.

How to Get Involved

When a book or other piece of art is challenged in a community, students are often caught in the middle. While students might be affected by a particular work, the challenge to that work is usually initiated by and decided upon by adults in the community who often believe they have the students' best interests at heart. So how

When a book is challenged, students can be caught in the middle between adults opposed to the work and those supporting it. Young people's voices should also be heard.

can students get more involved? What if they are the ones who have the objection, either to the book or to the removal of the book?

The best way for young people to get involved is by asking questions and sharing ideas. In particular, students should visit their school or local library and talk to the librarian about his or her experiences with book challenges. By finding out if their local library or school district has a policy for book challenges, and asking the librarian how that policy is administrated, young people can learn about the process and begin to understand why some books are challenged or banned in their community in particular. If there is a committee that reviews book challenges, students should ask whether they could attend one of the meetings to observe. If they would like to participate, students should request the opportunity to share their viewpoints so that the committee can benefit from their perspectives.

If students want to challenge the use of a book in a class, or if they believe that a book should not be available at their school or local library, they should first calmly discuss their concerns with their families and teachers. These adults, in turn, should be encouraged to read the book in question so they can fully understand the students' objections. Students and adults should then follow the rules set forth by the school district or library for filing an official challenge, and together, the community should come to some kind of compromise or resolution. Though objections to a book

131

can often lead to highly emotional situations, students and adults—whether they are challengers or defenders of a book—should remember that fair and safe outcomes are more often the result of calm and well-thought-out actions.

In addition to finding out how book challenges are dealt with in their communities, young people can also talk to their family members about book challenging so that they can have a better understanding of the opinions of their parents or guardians. Families should discuss whether some members support the banning of certain books and why. If they disagree with one another, they should discuss their opinions and together decide on a resolution as to how they will address the issue now and in the future.

Although young people can sometimes feel stifled by the rules set by teachers and guardians, many have also learned that these adults can be helpful guides when it comes to traversing the sometimes murky crossroads of literature and community. In discussing the impact of book challenges and censorship in the library setting, librarian Emma Boardman argues that the library is a place where young people should be free to explore, but that this exploration should be accompanied by discussion opportunities with and guidance from adults:

> What we tend to ignore in the debate within the library profession is that someone—teachers or parents—needs to discuss with young

people the materials they read. It is surely not a good idea to expose young people to alarming images and difficult issues without giving them a context in which to view them. The purpose of the library is to open the information environment, not to supply young people with an unending series of models for correct thought and behavior. But we need to let youth know that the difference between the expectations for their behavior, on one hand, and the goals of reading materials on the other.[7]

Books do not exist in a vacuum, and neither do readers. By discussing challenging issues, readers can better understand subjects that are new to them or that they do not agree with. Of course, some topics can cause emotions to run high. Rather than shy away from these areas, many people would argue that everyone can benefit from examining the reasons behind the furor. Perhaps, in the end, a challenge to a book can introduce everyone to new points of view.

1. What are some of the reasons why people try to ban books? Do you agree with these reasons? Why or why not?

2. It is often said that Mark Twain used comedy to criticize society. What do you think of these tactics? Are they effective? Why or why not?

3. Why did Mark Twain ask his wife, Livy, and his friend William Dean Howells to read his books before they were published?

4. Do you think that *The Adventures of Tom Sawyer* is appropriate to read in an eighth-grade class room? What about a fourth-grade classroom? Is it an appropriate book for a teacher to read to her first-grade students? Why or why not? What about *Adventures of Huckleberry Finn*? Why might your answers be different for each book?

5. Set up a mock courtroom with your class or club where you debate a challenge to either *The Adventures of Tom Sawyer* or *Adventures of Huckleberry Finn*. One half of the group should represent those trying to ban the novel; the other should represent those trying to allow access to the novel by everyone. How will you resolve the conflict?

6. Have there been any challenges to books in your area? How did this affect the community and how was the issue resolved? Do you agree or disagree with the outcome? Why?

339 B.C.—The philosopher Socrates is found guilty of being disrespectful of the gods and corrupting the youth of Athens through his teachings. He is sentenced to death by drinking hemlock. His death becomes a symbol of censorship in art and literature.

213 B.C.—Chinese emperor Shih Huang Ti has many books burned, including those of the scholar Confucius.

A.D. 8—The poet Ovid is banished from Rome, perhaps because he offended Emperor Augustus with his writings.

1450—Johannes Gutenberg invents the printing press in Germany.

1559—The Vatican publishes the *Index Librorum Prohibitorum*, or the Index of Forbidden Books.

1644—John Milton publishes *Areopagitica*.

1734—John Peter Zenger, the publisher of the *New York Weekly Journal*, is charged with libel after publishing articles criticizing the activities of New York's colonial governor, William Cosby. Alexander Hamilton successfully defends Zenger by arguing that the articles are not actually libelous because the information printed in them was true.

1788—The U.S. Constitution is ratified.

1818—Thomas Bowdler publishes the *Family Shakespeare*, in which he removes anything he considers lewd, immoral, or heretical.

1835—Samuel Langhorne Clemens, son of John and Jane Clemens, is born in Florida, Missouri, on November 30.

1845—Olivia (Livy) Langdon is born in Elmira, New York.

1847—John Clemens dies. Sam Clemens leaves school and becomes a newspaper apprentice.

1851—"A Gallant Fireman," Sam Clemens's first published story, appears in the *Hannibal Journal*, which is run by his brother, Orion.

1863—Clemens first uses the pseudonym "Mark Twain."

1870—Clemens marries Olivia Langdon and moves to Buffalo, New York. Livy's father, Jervis Langdon, dies. Langdon Clemens is born.

1872—Olivia Susan (Susy) Clemens is born. Langdon Clemens dies.

1873—Congress passes the Comstock Law, which makes it illegal to send anything obscene through the mail.

1874—Clara Langdon Clemens is born.

1876—*The Adventures of Tom Sawyer* is published.

1880—Jane (Jean) Lampton Clemens is born.

1885—*Adventures of Huckleberry Finn* is published. Within a month, the committee of the public library of Concord, Massachusetts, removes the novel from its shelves.

1891—Clemens family lives in Europe to save money.

1894—Clemens declares bankruptcy, and prepares for worldwide lecture tour to pay off debts. *The Tragedy of Pudd'nhead Wilson* is published.

1896—Susy Clemens dies.

1904—Livy Clemens dies in Florence, Italy.

1905—*Adventures of Huckleberry Finn* and *The Adventures of Tom Sawyer* are removed from the shelves of the Children's Department of the Brooklyn Public Library because the heroes of the books are thought to offer negative role models for young readers.

1909—Clara Clemens marries Ossip Gabrilowitsch. Jean Clemens dies.

1909—The National Association for the Advancement of Colored People (NAACP) is formed.

1910—Samuel Langhorne Clemens (aka Mark Twain) dies April 21.

1922—James Joyce's *Ulysses* is published.

1933—Federal court judge John Woolsey declares that *Ulysses* is not obscene.

1954—Supreme Court case, *Brown* v. *Board of Education*, outlaws racial segregation in schools.

1964—*Adventures of Huckleberry Finn* is removed from public school classrooms throughout Illinois after the state's chapter of the NAACP issues a challenge on the grounds that the book is racist.

1982—Through the *Island Trees Union Free School District's Board of Education* v. *Pico*, the Supreme Court determines that students do not "shed their constitutional rights to freedom of speech or expression at the schoolhouse gate" and that school libraries are a special place for the freedom of expression. Banned Books Week is created to educate the American public about the history of book banning and the potential impact it can have on one's culture and community.

2000—Southern Heights Ministerial Alliance, a coaltion of African-American ministers in Enid, Oklahoma, asks that *Adventures of Huckleberry Finn* be removed from required reading lists for juniors in the town's public high school.

Chapter Notes

Chapter 1:
Concord, Massachusetts, 1885, vs. Enid, Oklahoma, 2000

1. Ernest Hemingway, *Green Hills of Africa* (New York: Scribner's, 1935), p. 22.

2. "No 'Huckleberry Finn' for Concord," *Boston Globe*, March 17, 1885, p. 6.

3. Herbert N. Foerstel, *Banned in the U.S.A.: A Reference Guide to Book Censorship in Schools and Public Libraries*, revised and expanded edition (Westport, Conn.: Greenwood Press, 2002), p. 189.

4. Shelley Fisher Fishkin, *Was Huck Black? Mark Twain and African-American Voices*, e-book edition (New York: Oxford University Press, 1993), p. 4.

5. Michael McNutt, "'Huckleberry Finn' still stirs emotions," *The Daily Oklahoman*, November 25, 1999, p. 8A.

6. Arnold Hamilton, "'Huck Finn' debate flares up in Oklahoma: Some object to racial slur, want book off required list," *The Dallas Morning News*, December 30, 1999.

7. Michael McNutt, "Enid group challenges 'Huck Finn,'" *The Daily Oklahoman*, November 10, 1999, p. 18A.

8. Michael McNutt, "'Huckleberry Finn' still stirs emotions."

9. Ibid.

10. Michael McNutt, "Panel votes to drop 'Huck,'" *The Daily Oklahoman*, December 1, 1999, p. 14A.

11. Alvin Powell, "Fight over Huck Finn continues: Ed School professor wages battle for Twain classic," *The Harvard University Gazette*, September 28, 2000, <http://www.news.harvard.edu/gazette/2000/09.28/huckfinn.html> (May 1, 2006).

12. Jocelyn Chadwick, "Why Huck Finn Belongs in the Classroom," *Harvard Education Letter*, November/December 2000, <http://www.edletter.org/past/issues/2000-nd/huckfinn.shtml> (July 15, 2005).

13. Powell.

Chapter 2:
Why Ban Books?

1. Plato, "The Republic," *Great Dialogues of Plato*, W.H.D. Rouse, trans., Eric H. Warmington and Philip G. Rouse, eds. (New York: Penguin Group, 1956).

2. Frank Northen Magill, *Notable Poets: Magill's Choice* (Pasadena, Calif.: Salem Press, 1998), p. 823.

3. David Koeller, "China and East Asia Chronology: The Burning of the Books, 213BC," *WebChron: The Web Chronology Project*, 1999, <http://www.thenagain.info/WebChron//China/BookBurn.html> (March 12, 2006).

4. Herbert N. Foerstel, *Banned in the U.S.A.: A Reference Guide to Book Censorship in Schools and Public Libraries*, revised and expanded edition (Westport, Conn.: Greenwood Press, 2002), p. xv.

5. Edgar Lee Masters, "The New Star Chamber" (Chicago: Hammersmark Publishing Co., 1904), *Humanities*

Web, 1998–2006, <http://www.humanitiesweb.org/human. php?s=l&p=c&a=p&ID=21973&c=473> (April 21, 2007).

6. John Milton, "Areopagitica," *John Milton: The Complete English Poems*, Gordon Campbell, ed. (New York: Alfred A. Knopf, 1992), p. 578.

7. "Comstockery," Online Etymology Dictionary, November 2001, <http://www.etymonline.com/index.php? term=Comstockery> (March 19, 2006).

8. M. H. Abrams, *A Glossary of Literary Terms*, 6th ed. (New York: Harcourt Brace College Publishers, 1988), p. 202.

9. Hugh Ford, *Published in Paris* (New York: Pushcart Press, 1975), pp. 3–33.

10. "100 Best Novels," The Modern Library, 2003, <http://www.randomhouse.com/modernlibrary/100bestnov els.html> (March 26, 2006).

11. Christine Gibson, "Pornography or Great Literature?" *American Heritage.com*, 2006, <http://www. americanheritage.com/entertainment/articles/web/20051206 -james-joyce-ulysses-censorship-sex-pornography-little- review-random-house-smoot-hawley-tariff-act-john- woolsey-customs.shtml> (March 26, 2006).

12. Esther Lobardi, "Banning Ulysses," *About.com*, 2006, <http://classiclit.about.com/od/bannedliteratur1/a/aa_ulysses _4.htm> (March 26, 2006).

13. Ibid.

14. Jerry Goldman, "Roth v. United States," *OYEZ, U.S. Supreme Court Multimedia*, 1996–2005, <http://www.oyez. org/oyez/resource/case/338/> (March 25, 2006).

15. Jerry Goldman, "Miller v. California," *OYEZ, U.S. Supreme Court Multimedia*, 1996–2005, <http://www.oyez. org/oyez/resource/case/247/> (March 25, 2006).

16. Jerry Goldman, "Board of Education v. Pico," *OYEZ, U.S. Supreme Court Multimedia*, 1996–2005, <http://www. oyez.org/oyez/resource/case/1060/> (April 8, 2006).

17. Maureen Harrison and Steve Gilbert, *Landmark Decisions of the United States Supreme Court* (Beverley Hills, Calif.: Excellent Books, 1991), p. 162.

18. "Notable First Amendment Court Cases," *American Library Association*, 2007,<https://www.ala.org/ala/oif/first amendment/courtcases/courtcases.htm> (April 21, 2007).

19. Harrison and Gilbert, p. 167.

20. Donald J. Rogers, *Banned! Book Censorship in Schools* (New York: Julian Messner, 1988), p. 3.

21. Ezra Bowen, "A Debate Over 'Dumbing Down'," *Time Magazine*, December 3, 1984, <http://www.time.com/ time/magazine/article/0,9171,923778-2,00.html> (April 23, 2007).

22. "The 100 Most Frequently Challenged Books 1990–2000," American Library Association, 2005, <http://www.ala.org/ala/oif/bannedbooksweek/bbwlinks/10 0mostfrequently.htm> (March 25, 2006).

23. Ray Bradbury, *Fahrenheit 451* (New York: Ballantine Books, 1953), p. 57.

142

24. Ray Bradbury, "Author's Afterword," *Fahrenheit 451* (New York: Ballantine Books, 1979), p. 165.

25. Ibid.

26. Ibid., p. 167.

27. "Challenged and Banned Books," American Library Association, 2005, <http://www.ala.org/ala/oif/bannedbooks week/challengedbanned/challengedbanned.htm> (March 25, 2006).

28. "Why Banned Books Week?" American Library Association, 2005, <http://www.ala.org/ala/oif/bannedbooks week/backgroundb/background.htm> (March 25, 2006).

Chapter 3:
Sam Clemens and Mark Twain: One Man, Two Identities

1. Fred Kaplan, *The Singular Mark Twain: A Biography* (New York: Anchor Books, 2003), p. 106.

2. Ibid., 106–107.

3. Mark Twain, *The Autobiography of Mark Twain*, Charles Neider, ed. (New York: Perennial Classics, 1959), pp. 1–2.

4. Ibid.

5. Ibid., p. 39.

6. Ibid., pp. 7–8.

7. Kaplan, p. 32.

8. Ibid., pp. 42–43.

9. Justin Kaplan, *Mr. Clemens and Mark Twain* (New York: Simon and Schuster, 1966), p. 231.

10. Philip Fisher, "Mark Twain," *Columbia Literary History of the United States*, Martha Banta, Terence Martin, David Minter, Marjorie Perloff, Daniel B. Shea, Emory Elliott, Houston A. Baker, Nina Baym, and Sacvan Bercovitch, eds. (New York: Columbia University Press, 1988), p. 632, *Questia*, <http://www.questia.com/PM.qst?a=o&d=42488703> (April 22, 2007).

11. Justin Kaplan, p. 77.

12. Fred Kaplan, p. 231.

13. Ibid., p. 232; and Twain, *The Autobiography of Mark Twain*, pp. 241–242.

14. "Samuel Clemens/Mark Twain: 1835–1910," The Mark Twain House and Museum, 2004, <http://www.marktwainhouse.org/theman/timeline.shtml> (July 13, 2005).

15. Twain, *The Autobiography of Mark Twain*, p. 240.

16. Justin Kaplan, p. 181.

17. Fred Kaplan, pp. 311–312.

18. Ibid., p. 319.

19. Twain, *The Autobiography of Mark Twain*, pp. 242–243.

20. Jim Zwick, "Mark Twain on Book Banning: *Huck Finn* to *Eve's Diary*," *Mark Twain*, Jim Zwick, ed., 1995–2006, <http://www.boondocksnet.com/twainwww/twain_banned.html> (July 13, 2005).

21. Jim Zwick, "Beyond Book Banning: Censorship of Mark Twain's Political Writings," *Mark Twain*, Jim Zwick, ed., 1995–2006, <http://www.boondocksnet.com/twain

www/essays/beyond_book_banning020921.html>
(September 10, 2006). See also Jim Zwick, "The *Real* 'United
States of Lyncherdom': An Interview with Terry Oggel,"
Mark Twain, Jim Zwick, ed., 1995–2006, <http://www.
boondocksnet.com/twainwww/essays/oggel_lyncherdom02
0114.html> (September 10, 2006).

22. Fred Kaplan, p. 512.

23. Twain, *The Autobiography of Mark Twain*,
p. 486.

24. Fred Kaplan, pp. 654–655.

Chapter 4:
The Adventures of Tom Sawyer

1. Mark Twain. *The Adventures of Tom Sawyer* (New
York: New American Library, 1959), p. 1.

2. Ibid., p. 18

3. Ibid., p. 21.

4. Ibid.

5. Ibid., pp. 21–22.

6. Ibid., p. 22.

7. Ibid., pp. 89–90.

8. Ibid., p. 195.

9. Ibid., p. 219.

10. Justin Kaplan, *Mr. Clemens and Mark Twain* (New
York: Simon and Schuster, 1966), p. 178.

11. Mark Twain, *The Autobiography of Mark Twain*, Charles Neider, ed. (New York: Perennial Classics, 1959), p. 347.

12. Justin Kaplan, p. 180.

13. Ibid.

14. Twain, *The Adventures of Tom Sawyer*, p. 5.

15. Ibid., p. 219.

16. Stephen Railton, "Getting Tom to Market," *Mark Twain in His Times*, 1996–2004, <http://etext.virginia.edu/railton/tomsawye/tomcomp.html> (April 10, 2006).

17. Fred Kaplan, *The Singular Mark Twain: A Biography* (New York: Anchor Books, 2003), p. 327.

18. "Review," *British Quarterly Review*, October 1876, Stephen Railton, ed., *Mark Twain in His Times*, 1996–2004, <http://etext.virginia.edu/railton/tomsawye/britqrev.html> (September 10, 2006).

19. "Review," *Athenaeum*, June 24, 1876, Stephen Railton, ed., *Mark Twain in His Times*, 1996–2004, <http://etext.virginia.edu/railton/tomsawye/athenaeu.html> (September 10, 2006).

20. William Dean Howells, "Review," *The Atlantic Monthly*, May 1876, Stephen Railton, ed., *Mark Twain in His Times*, 1996–2004, <http://etext.virginia.edu/railton/tomsawye/atlantts.html> (April 10, 2006).

21. Charles Dudley Warner, "Review," *Hartford Daily Courant*, December 27, 1876, Stephen Railton, ed., *Mark Twain in His Times*, 1996–2004, <http://etext.virginia.edu/railton/tomsawye/hartcour.html> (September 10, 2006).

22. Edgar Lee Masters, "Mark Twain," *Mark Twain: A Portrait* (New York: Charles Scribner's Sons, 1938), in Mark Twain, *The Adventures of Tom Sawyer*, e-book edition (Philadelphia, Pa.: Running Press, 1987), p. 158.

Chapter 5:
Adventures of Huckleberry Finn

1. Mark Twain, *Adventures of Huckleberry Finn*, Henry Nash Smith, ed. (Boston: Houghton Mifflin Company, 1958), p. 3.

2. Ibid., p. 78.

3. Ibid., p. 92.

4. Ibid., pp. 97–98.

5. Ibid., p. 99.

6. Philip Fisher, "Mark Twain," *Columbia Literary History of the United States*, Martha Banta, Terence Martin, David Minter, Marjorie Perloff, Daniel B. Shea, Emory Elliott, Houston A. Baker, Nina Baym, and Sacvan Bercovitch, eds. (New York: Columbia University Press, 1988), p. 639, *Questia*, <http://www.questia.com/PM.qst?a= o&d=42488715> (April 22, 2007).

7. Twain, *Adventures of Huckleberry Finn*, pp. 188–189.

8. Ibid., p. 245.

9. Ibid., p. 38.

10. Ibid., p. 180

11. Lionel Trilling, "*Huckleberry Finn*, 1948," *The Moral Obligation to Be Intelligent*, Leon Wieseltier, ed. (New York: Farrar, Straus & Giroux, 2000), p. 144.

12. Jonathan Arac, *Huckleberry Finn as Idol and Target: The Functions of Criticism in Our Time* (Madison, Wis.: University of Wisconsin Press, 1997), p. 31.

13. Ibid., p. 34.

14. Fred Kaplan, *The Singular Mark Twain: A Biography* (New York: Anchor Books, 2003), p. 33.

15. Forrest G. Robinson, "Mark Twain 1835–1910: A Brief Biography," *A Historical Guide to Mark Twain*, Shelly Fisher Fishkin, ed. (New York: Oxford University Press, 2002), p. 33.

16. Fisher, p. 644.

17. Twain, *Adventures of Huckleberry Finn*, p. 2.

18. Shelley Fisher Fishkin, *Was Huck Black? Mark Twain and African-American Voices*, e-book edition (New York: Oxford University Press, 1993), p. 116.

19. Justin Kaplan, *Mr. Clemens and Mark Twain* (New York: Simon and Schuster, 1966), p. 197.

20. Ibid.

21. Twain, *Adventures of Huckleberry Finn*, p. 3.

22. Justin Kaplan, p. 267.

23. Fred Kaplan, pp. 410–411

24. Ibid.

25. Trilling, pp. 138–139.

Chapter 6:
The War Against Twain

1. "The 100 Most Frequently Challenged Books 1990–2000," American Library Association, 2005, <http://www.ala.org/ala/oif/bannedbooksweek/bbwlinks/100most frequently.htm> (April 28, 2006).

2. "No 'Huckleberry Finn' for Concord," *Boston Globe*, March 17, 1885, *Mark Twain*, Jim Zwick, ed., 1995–2006, <http://www.boondocksnet.com/twaintexts/huck_banned_ bg18850317.html> (February 6, 2006).

3. Ibid.

4. *Life*, April 9, 1885, p. 202, "Mark Twain's *Huckleberry Finn*: Text, Illustrations, and Early Reviews," Virginia H. Cope, ed., <http://etext.lib.virginia.edu/twain/ life2.html> (May 4, 2006).

5. Justin Kaplan, *Mr. Clemens and Mark Twain* (New York: Simon and Schuster, 1966), p. 268.

6. Ibid., p. 269.

7. Mark Twain, "Letter to Asa Don Dickinson, November 21, 1905," *New York Times*, November 2, 1935.

8. Ibid.

9. Jim Zwick, "Banned Books and American Culture," *Mark Twain*, Jim Zwick, ed., 1995–2006, <http://www.boon docksnet.com/twainwww/essays/banned_books9709.html> (July 13, 2005).

10. "Mission," National Association for the Advancement of Colored People, 2006, <http://www. naacp.org/about/mission/index.htm> (May 5, 2006).

11. Zwick, "Banned Books and American Culture."

12. Shelley Fisher Fishkin, *Was Huck Black? Mark Twain and African-American Voices*, e-book edition (New York: Oxford University Press, 1993), p. 107.

13. Leonard Buder, "'Huck Finn' Barred As Textbook by City," *The New York Times*, September 12, 1957, *Mark Twain Quotations, Newspaper Collections, & Related Resources*, Barbara Schmidt, ed., <http://www.twainquotes.com/19570912.html> (May 5, 2006).

14. Ibid.

15. Jonathan Arac, *Huckleberry Finn as Idol and Target: The Functions of Criticism in Our Time* (Madison, Wis.: University of Wisconsin Press, 1997), p. 66.

16. John S. Simmons and Eliza T. Dresang, *School Censorship in the 21st Century: A Guide for Teachers and School Library Media Specialists* (Newark, Del.: International Reading Association, 2001), p. 156.

17. Ibid.

18. Nancy Kravitz, *Censorship and the School Library Media Center* (Westport, Conn.: Libraries Unlimited, A Division of Greenwood Publishing Group, Inc., 2002), p. 84.

19. Ibid.

20. "Federal appeals court allows 'Huck Finn' to remain on school's reading list," Associated Press, October 20, 1998, *The Freedom Forum*, <http://www.freedomforum.org/templates/document.asp?documentID=9103> (April 22, 2007).

21. Herbert N. Foerstel, *Banned in the U.S.A.: A Reference Guide to Book Censorship in Schools and Public Libraries*, revised and expanded edition (Westport, Conn.: Greenwood Press, 2002), p. 193.

22. Ibid.

23. Arac, p. viii.

24. Ibid., p. 10.

25. Fishkin, 107.

Chapter 7:
Defending *Tom Sawyer* and *Huck Finn*

1. *St. Louis Post-Dispatch*, March 17, 1885, p. 4, "Mark Twain's *Huckleberry Finn*: Text, Illustrations, and Early Reviews," Virginia H. Cope, ed., <http://etext.lib.virginia.edu/twain/louispd.html> (February 2, 2006).

2. San Francisco *Chronicle*, March 29, 1885, p. 4, "Mark Twain's *Huckleberry Finn*: Text, Illustrations, and Early Reviews," Virginia H. Cope, ed., <http://etext.lib.virginia.edu/twain/sfchron2.html> (February 2, 2006).

3. Ibid.

4. "'*Huckleberry Finn*' and His Critics," *Atlanta Constitution*, May 26, 1885, University of Virginia Library, 1996–2004, <http://etext.lib.virginia.edu/railton/huckfinn/atlanta.html> (April 25, 2007).

5. Fred Kaplan, *The Singular Mark Twain* (New York: Anchor Books, 2003), pp. 410–411.

6. Mark Twain, *The Autobiography of Mark Twain*, Charles Neider, ed. (New York: Perennial Classics, 1959), p. 8.

7. Kaplan, p. 411.

8. Jim Zwick, "Banned Books and American Culture," *Mark Twain*, Jim Zwick, ed. 1995–2006, <http://www.boondocksnet.com/twainwww/essays/banned_books9709.html> (July 13, 2005).

9. Shelley Fisher Fishkin, "Mark Twain and Race," *A Historical Guide to Mark Twain*, Shelly Fisher Fishkin, ed. (New York: Oxford University Press, 2002), p. 137.

10. Toni Morrison, *Playing in the Dark: Whiteness and the Literary Imagination* (Cambridge, Mass.: Harvard University Press, 1992), p. 54.

11. For more information about possible activities or discussion questions, see "Culture Shock—*Huck Finn* in Context: A Teaching Guide," WGBH Educational Foundation, 1999, <http://www.pbs.org/wgbh/cutureshock/teachers/huck/index.html> (September 9, 2006).

Chapter 8:
Closing Arguments

1. Mark Twain, *The Autobiography of Mark Twain*, Charles Neider, ed. (New York: Perennial Classics, 1959), pp. 39–40.

2. Edna M. Boardman, *Censorship: The Problem that Won't Go Away* (Worthington, Ohio: Linworth Publishing, Inc., 1993), p. 3.2.

3. John S. Simmons and Eliza T. Dresang, *School Censorship in the 21st Century: A Guide for Teachers and School Library Media Specialists* (Newark, Del.: International Reading Association, 2001), p. 186.

4. Ibid.

5. Jim Zwick, "Banned Books and American Culture," *Mark Twain*, Jim Zwick, ed., 1995–2006, <http://www.boon docksnet.com/twainwww/essays/banned_books9709.html> (July 13, 2005).

6. Jocelyn Chadwick, "Why Huck Finn Belongs in the Classroom," *Harvard Education Letter*, November/December 2000, <http://www.edletter.org/past/issues/2000nd/huck finn.shtml> (July 15, 2005).

7. Boardman, p. 3.2.

Selected works of Mark Twain

Glossary

abolitionists—People who believed that slavery should be abolished.

antebellum—Before the American Civil War.

apprentice—An assistant, usually someone learning a trade.

Banned Books Week—The weekly celebration of freedom of speech that takes place each year in the last week of September. Banned Books Week is sponsored by a coalition of organizations that includes the American Library Association.

Bill of Rights—The document that outlines the basic civil liberties of American citizens through the first ten amendments to the Constitution.

bowdlerize—To edit by removing passages considered offensive. The term comes from the name of Thomas Bowdler.

Index Librorum Prohibitorum—The Index of Forbidden Books, published by the Vatican in 1559. It consisted of works of philosophy and theology. A version of it is still in existence today.

mark twain—Two fathoms, or twelve feet, in riverboat vocabulary. The phrase used to denote the line between safe and dangerous waters for a boat along the river.

National Association for the Advancement of Colored People (NAACP)—Organization founded in New York City in 1909 by a multiracial group of activists that seeks to ensure the political, educational, social, and economic equality of rights of all persons and to eliminate racial hatred and racial discrimination.

Star Chamber—A small court established by the British government in the seventeenth century. It had no jury and tried printers who were suspected of printing works criticizing King Charles I.

subscription book—A book for which readers paid in advance. Usually publishers tried to sell a certain number of subscriptions before the book was printed.

Books

Bloom, Harold, editor. *Mark Twain*. New York: Chelsea House Publishers, 2006.

Day, Nancy. *Censorship, or Freedom of Expression?* Minneapolis, Minn.: Lerner Publications Company, 2001.

Foerstel, Herbert N. *Banned in the U.S.A.: A Reference Guide to Book Censorship in Schools and Public Libraries*. Revised and Expanded Edition. Westport, Conn.: Greenwood Press, 2002.

McArthur, Debra. *Mark Twain*. New York: Marshall Cavendish, 2006.

Roleff, Tamara, editor. *Censorship: Opposing Viewpoints*. San Diego: Greenhaven Press, 2002.

Internet Addresses

American Library Association—Banned Books Week site
<http://www.ala.org/ala/oif/bannedbooksweek/banned booksweek.htm>

Mark Twain House
<http://www.marktwainhouse.org/>

National Association for the Advancement of Colored People
<http://www.naacp.org>

Index

Index

159